Usborne

Penc
& Paper Games

Written by Simon Tudhope
Designed by Marc Maynard
Edited by Sam Taplin

Contents

1	Hangman
12	Stepping stones
24	Four in a row
36	Minefield
47	Os and Xs
57	Hive
67	Strike out
77	Code breaker
86	Sharp shooter
98	Battleships
109	Caterpillar
119	Shooting stars
127	Super Os and Xs
137	Crossed words
149	Boxes
157	Triangles
167	Treasure hunter
176	Sprouts
186	OXO
194	Pair them up

Hangman instructions

1 Each game has a subject, such as monsters. Player 1 thinks of a word that fits the subject, then marks it in the space with a dash for each letter.

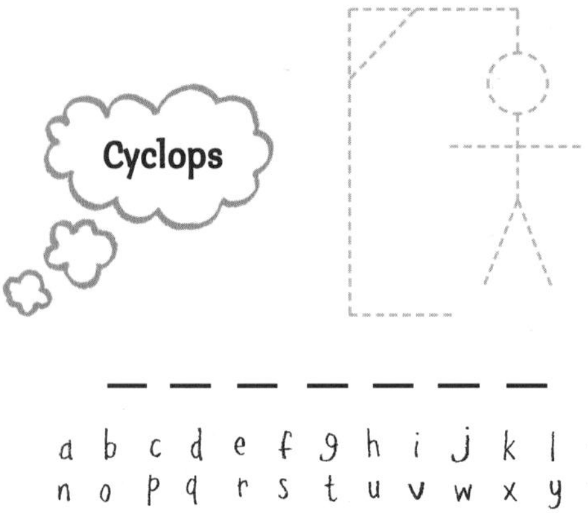

2 Player 2 then calls out a letter and crosses it off the alphabet. If the letter is in the word, Player 1 writes it above the correct dash.

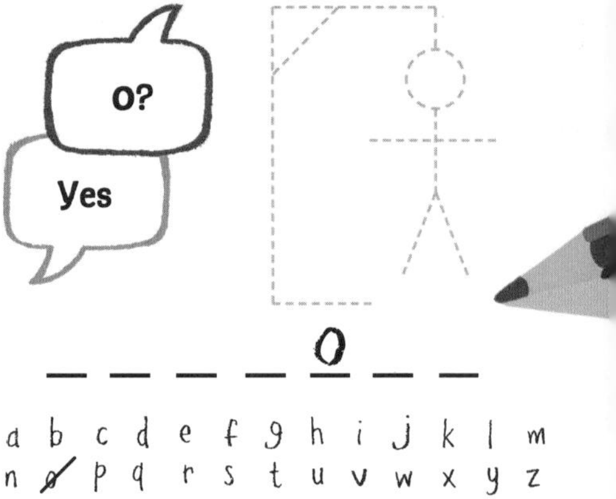

3 If the letter isn't in the word, Player 1 fills in one line of the hangman picture.

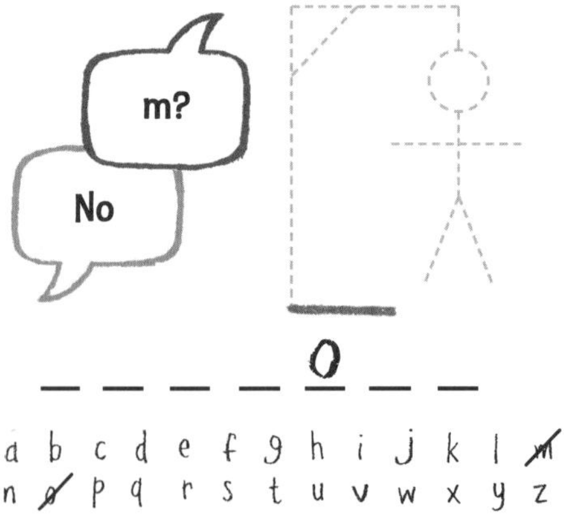

4 There are ten parts to the hangman picture. Player 2 wins if they spell the word before all the parts have been drawn. Player 1 won this game.

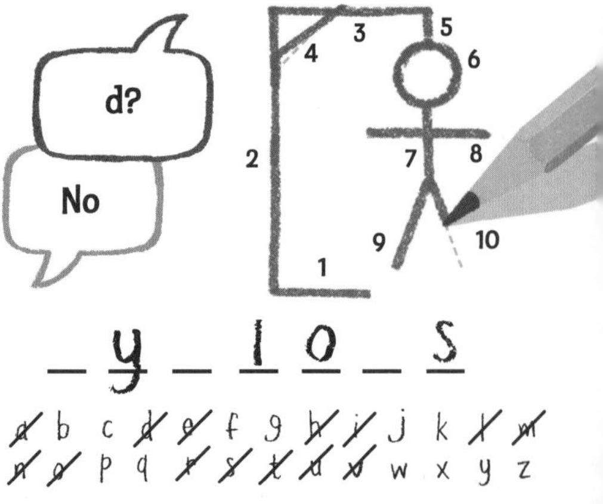

Hangman

2

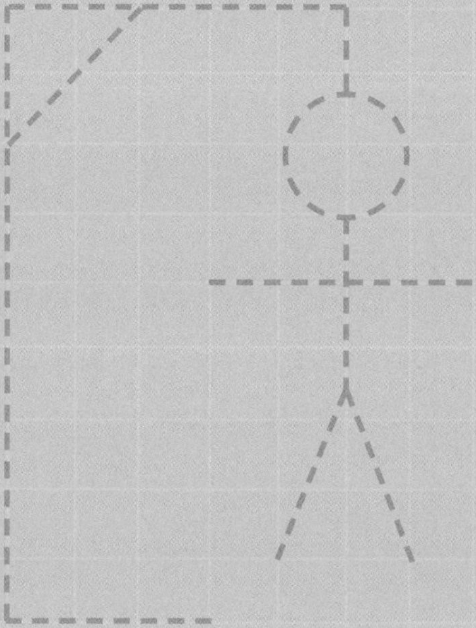

Your subject is MONSTERS.

Use the space below for your word.

a	b	c	d	e	f	g	h	i	j	k	l	m
n	o	p	q	r	s	t	u	v	w	x	y	z

Hangman

3

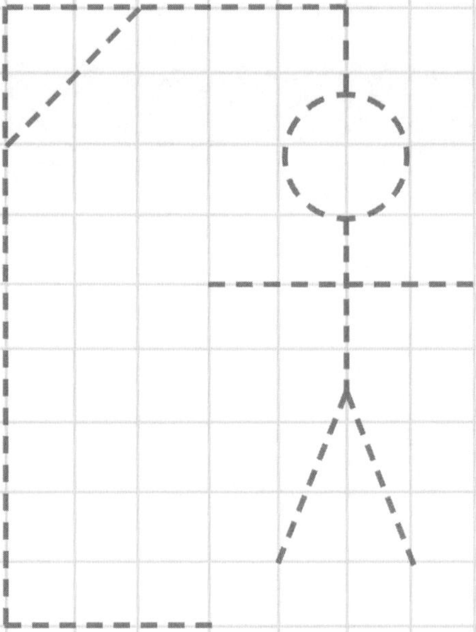

Your subject is ANIMALS.
Use the space below for your word.

a	b	c	d	e	f	g	h	i	j	k	l	m
n	o	p	q	r	s	t	u	v	w	x	y	z

Hangman

4

Your subject is SPACE.

Use the space below for your word.

a	b	c	d	e	f	g	h	i	j	k	l	m
n	o	p	q	r	s	t	u	v	w	x	y	z

Hangman

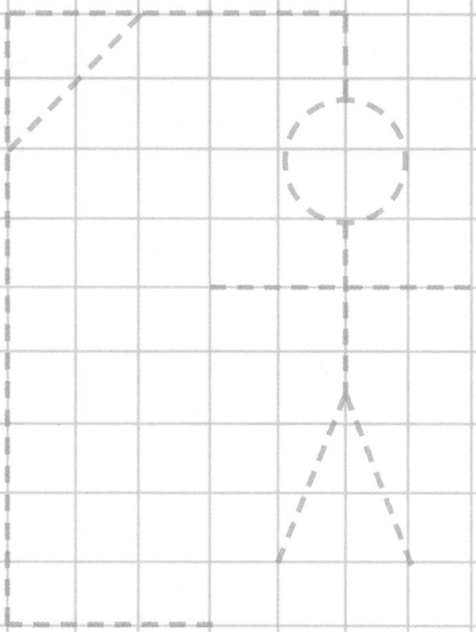

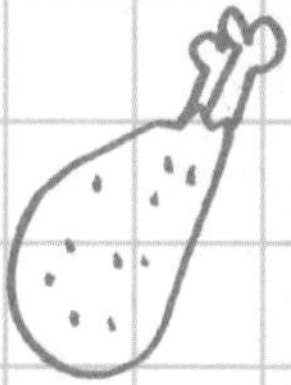

Your subject is FOOD AND DRINK.
Use the space below for your word.

a	b	c	d	e	f	g	h	i	j	k	l	m
n	o	p	q	r	s	t	u	v	w	x	y	z

Hangman

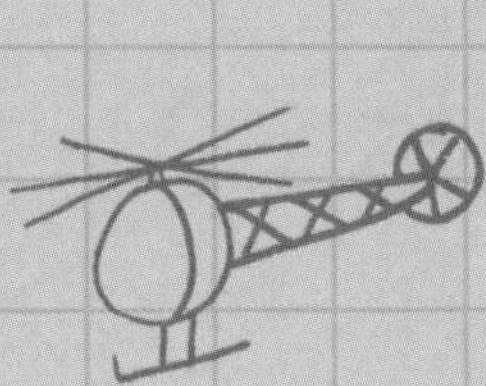

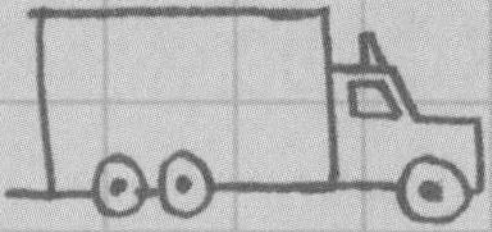

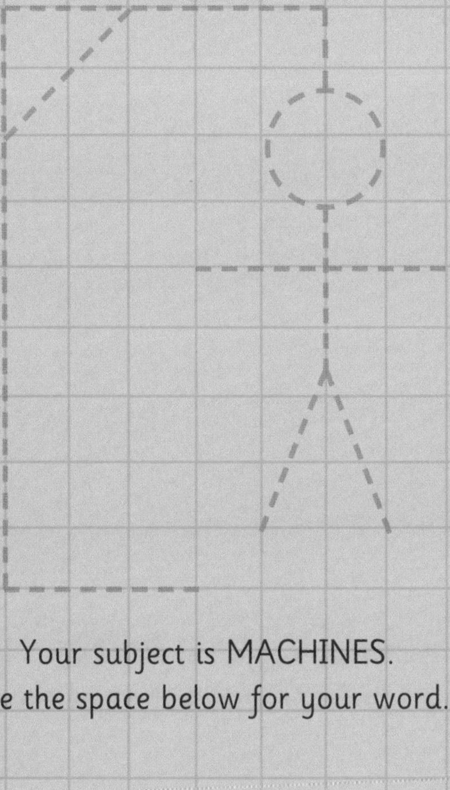

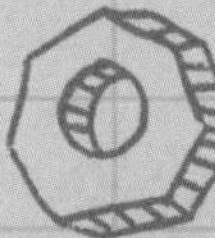

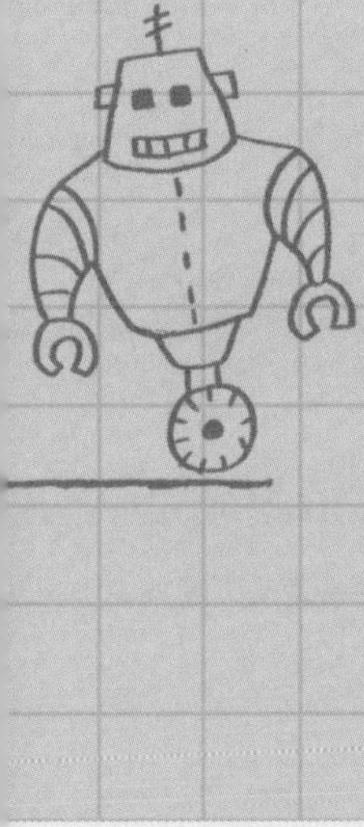

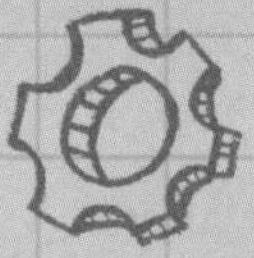

Your subject is MACHINES.
Use the space below for your word.

a	b	c	d	e	f	g	h	i	j	k	l	m
n	o	p	q	r	s	t	u	v	w	x	y	z

Hangman

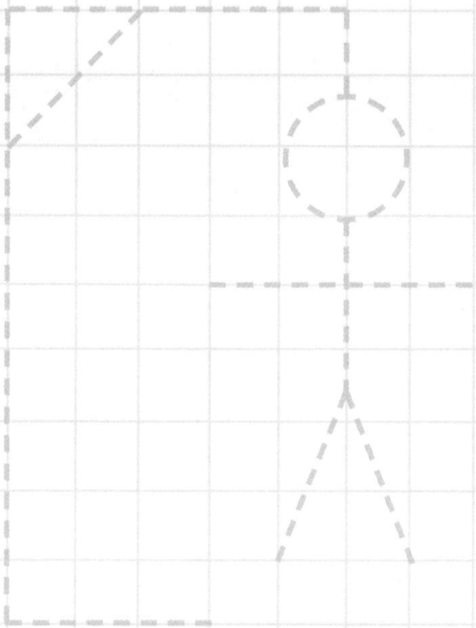

Your subject is NATURE.
Use the space below for your word.

a	b	c	d	e	f	g	h	i	j	k	l	m
n	o	p	q	r	s	t	u	v	w	x	y	z

Hangman

8

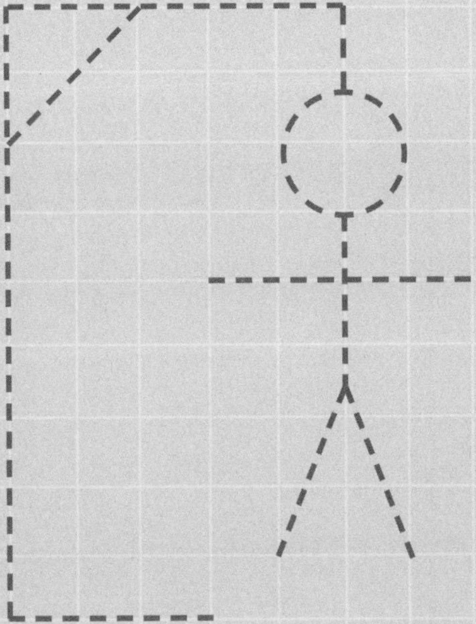

Your subject is AROUND THE WORLD.
Use the space below for your word.

a	b	c	d	e	f	g	h	i	j	k	l	m
n	o	p	q	r	s	t	u	v	w	x	y	z

Hangman

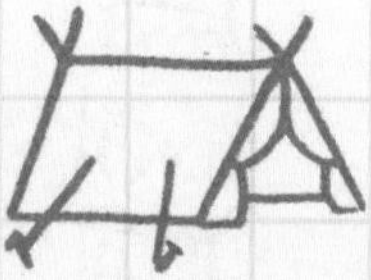

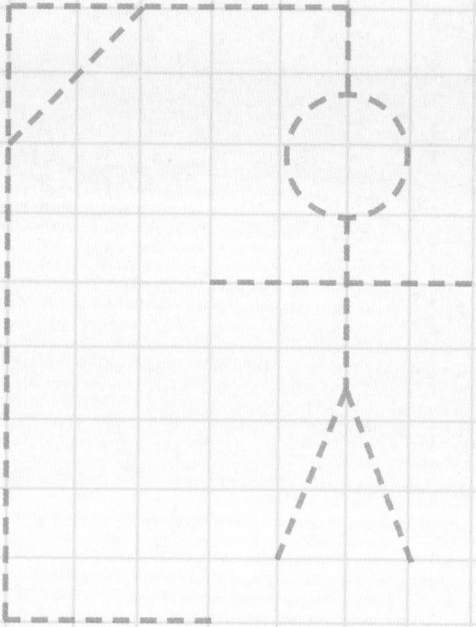

Your subject is TRAVEL.
Use the space below for your word.

a	b	c	d	e	f	g	h	i	j	k	l	m
n	o	p	q	r	s	t	u	v	w	x	y	z

Hangman

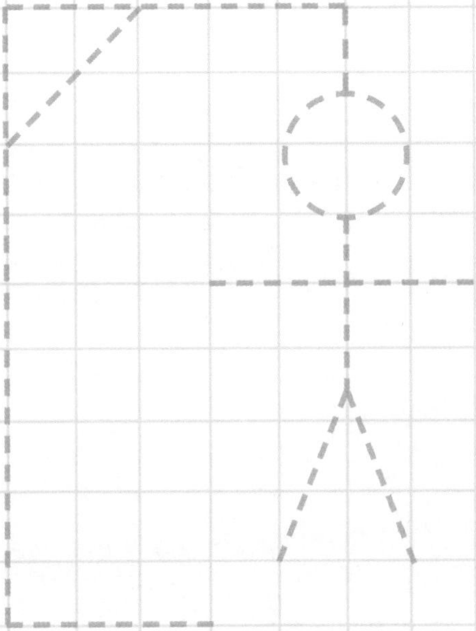

Your subject is UNDER THE SEA.
Use the space below for your word.

a	b	c	d	e	f	g	h	i	j	k	l	m
n	o	p	q	r	s	t	u	v	w	x	y	z

Hangman

11

Your subject is SPORTS.
Use the space below for your word.

a	b	c	d	e	f	g	h	i	j	k	l	m
n	o	p	q	r	s	t	u	v	w	x	y	z

Stepping stones instructions

1 Player 1 starts by connecting two of the purple dots together using a horizontal or vertical straight line.

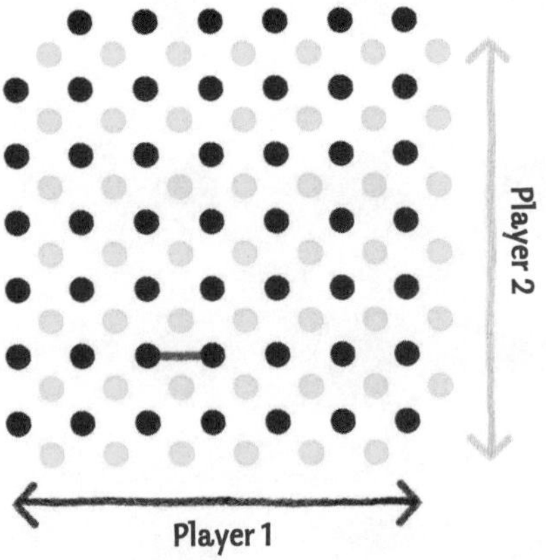

2 Player 2 then connects two of the yellow dots together using a horizontal or vertical straight line.

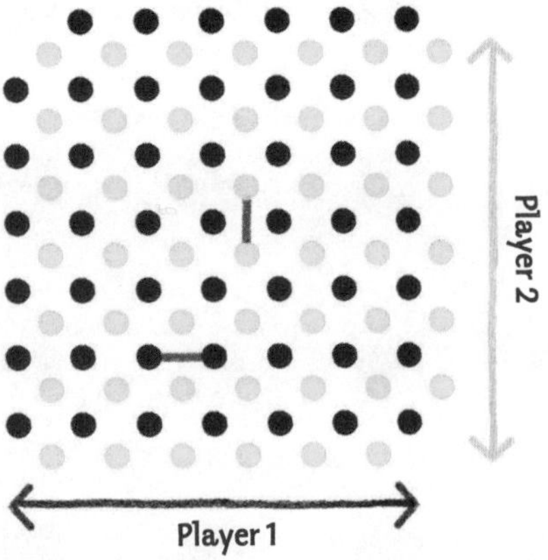

3 Taking turns, connect two of your dots anywhere on the grid. But you can't cross a line that's already been made.

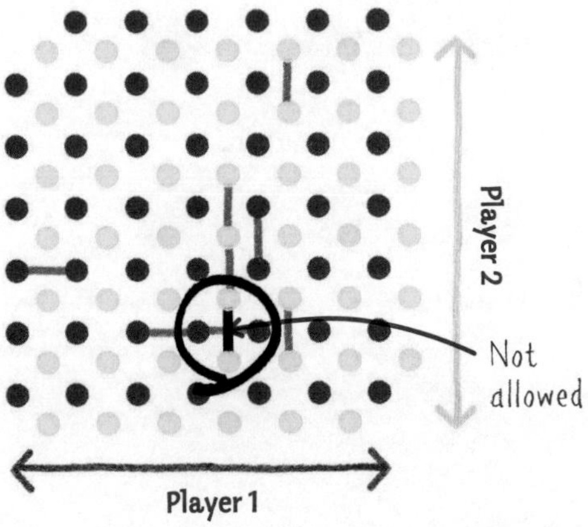

4 The first player to cross the grid is the winner. Player 1's chain must cross from side to side, and Player 2's from top to bottom.

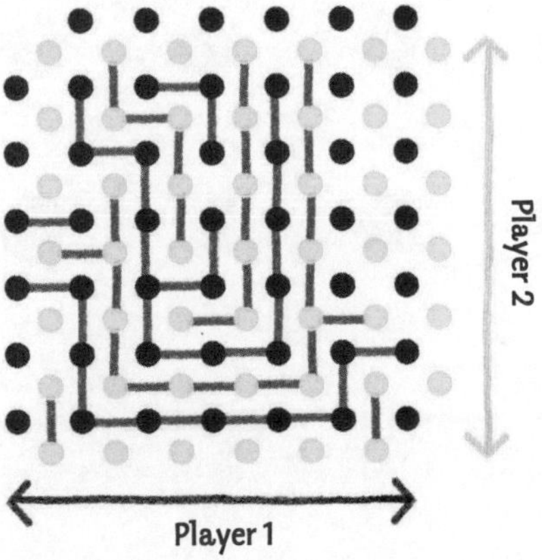

(Player 1 won this game.)

Stepping stones

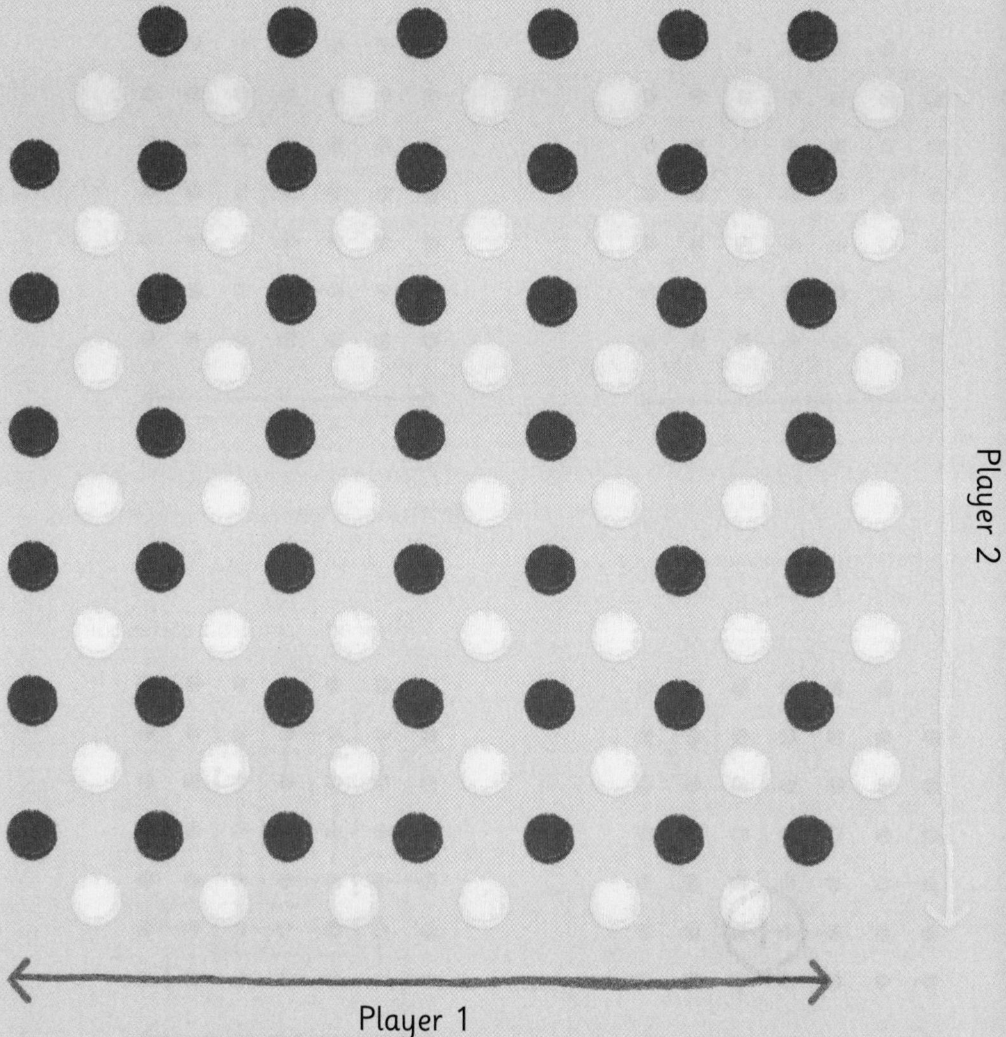

Stepping stones

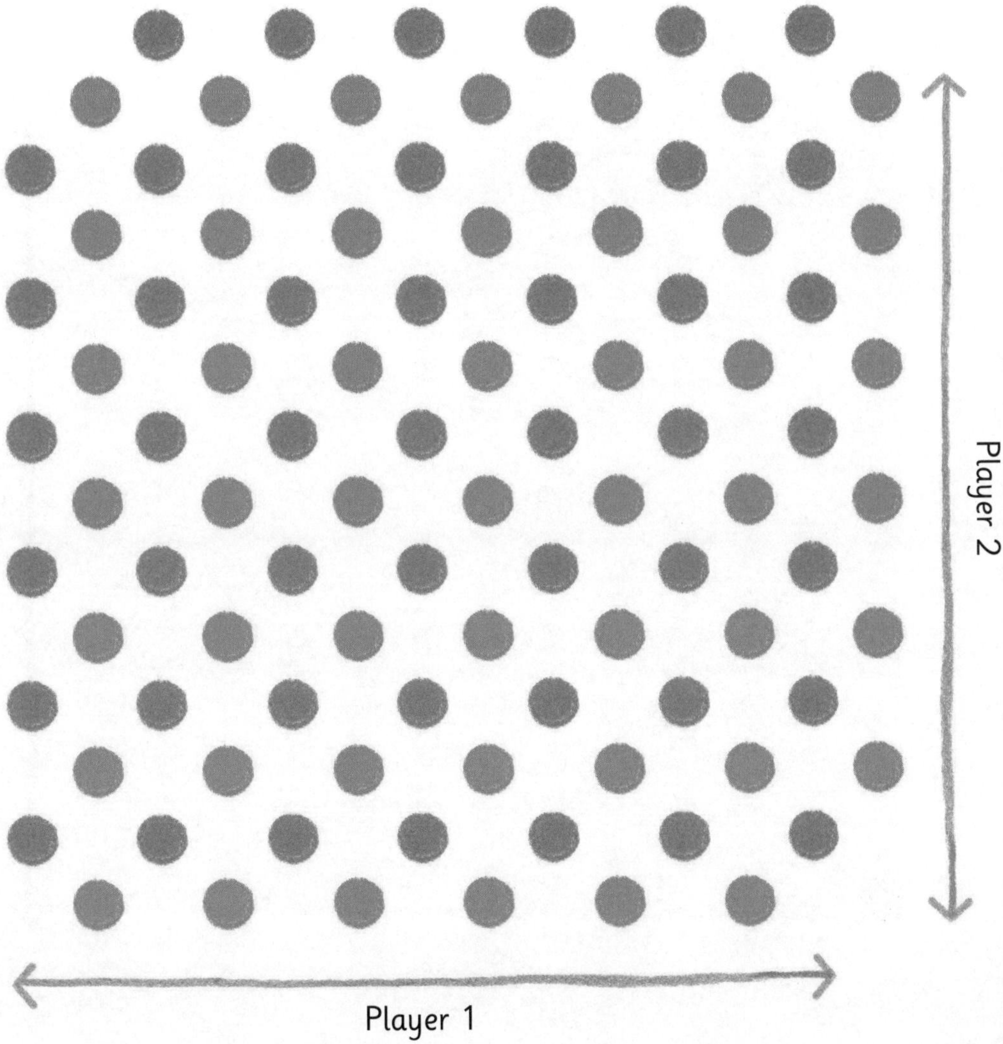

Stepping stones

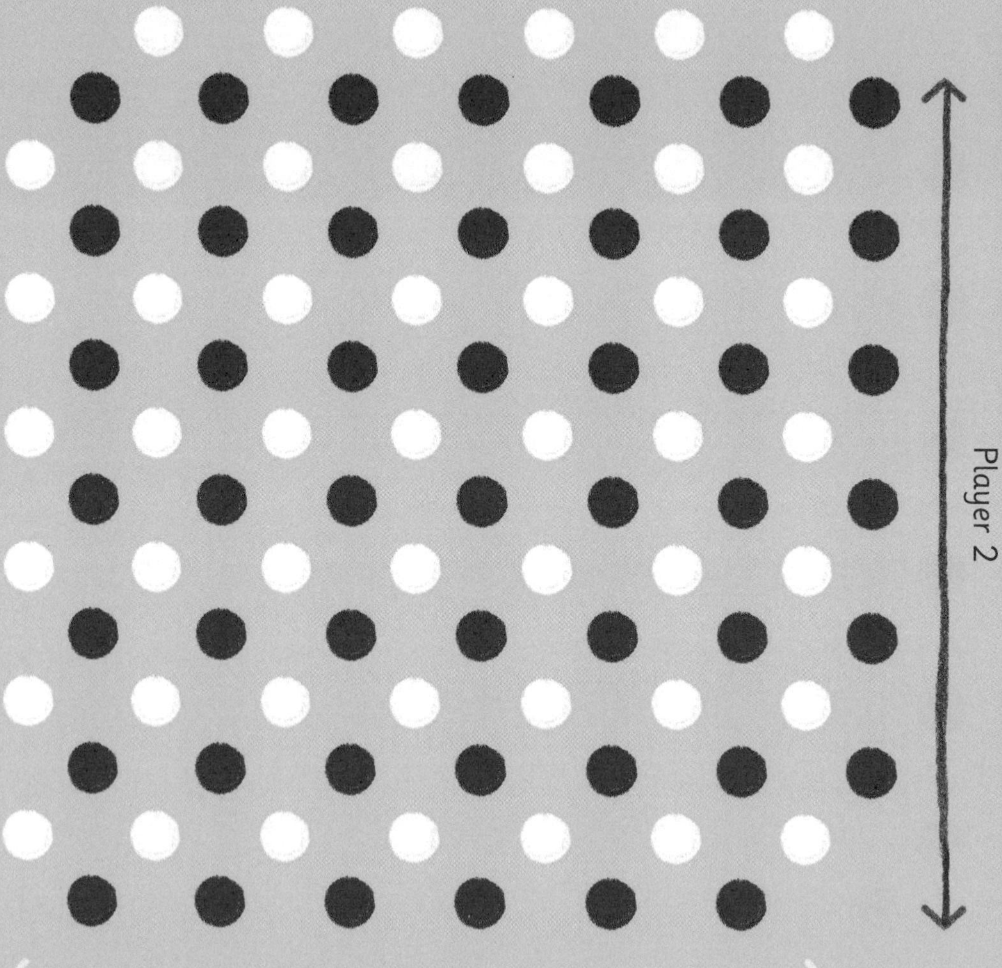

Stepping stones

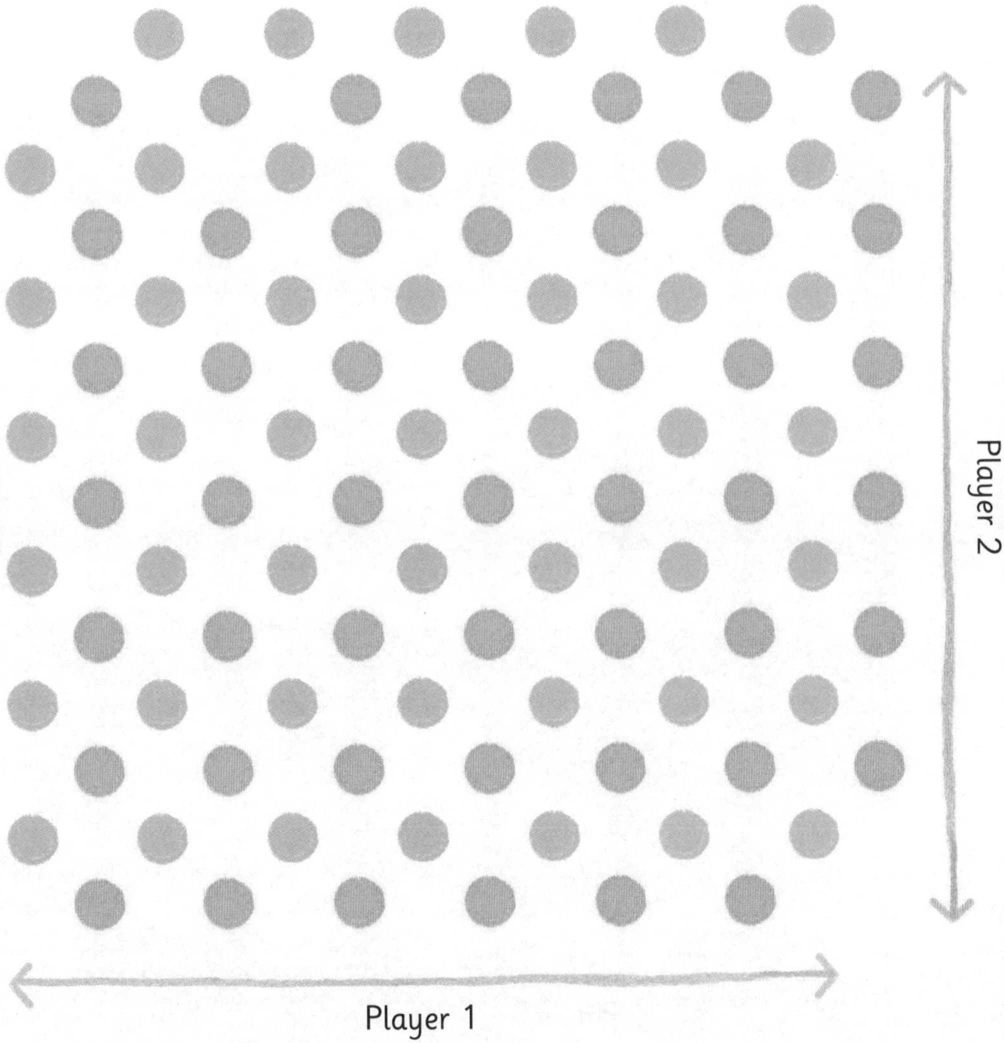

Stepping stones

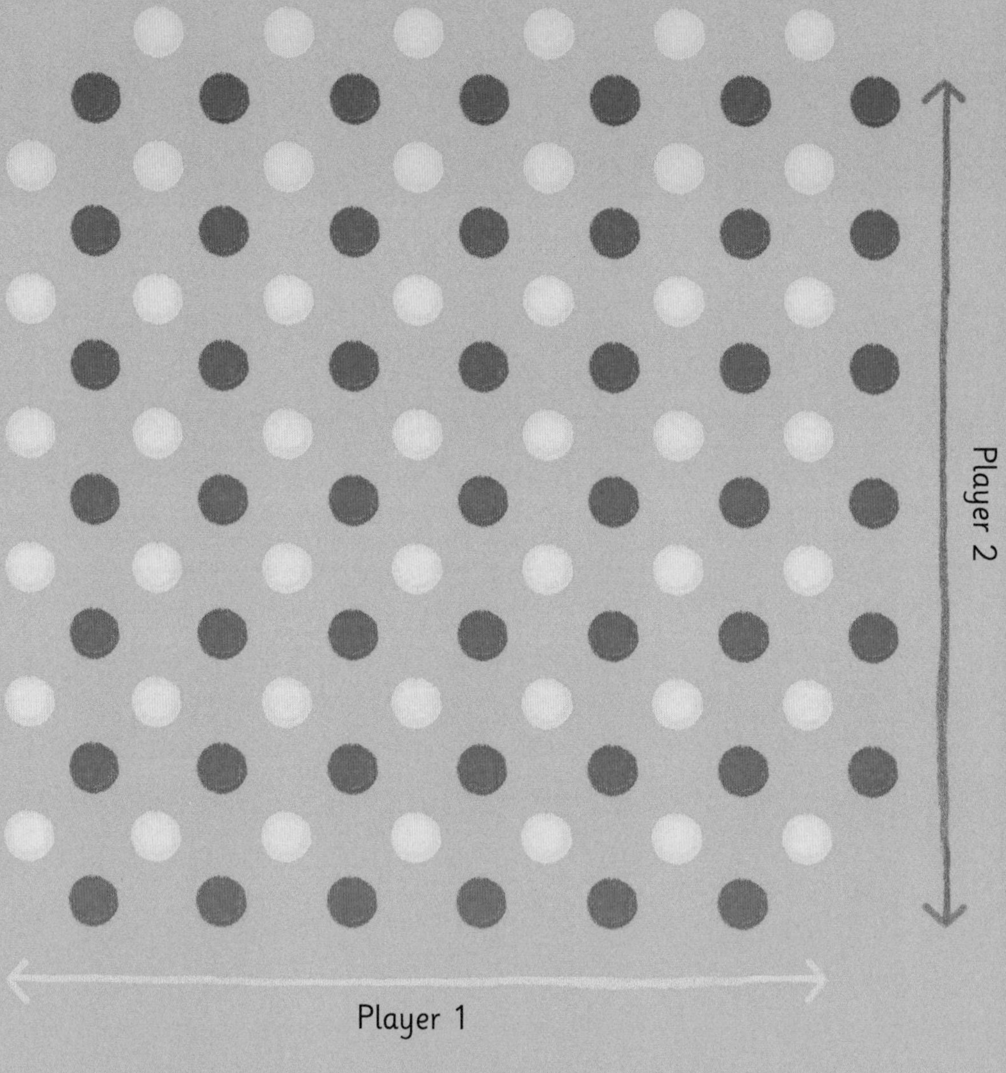

Stepping stones

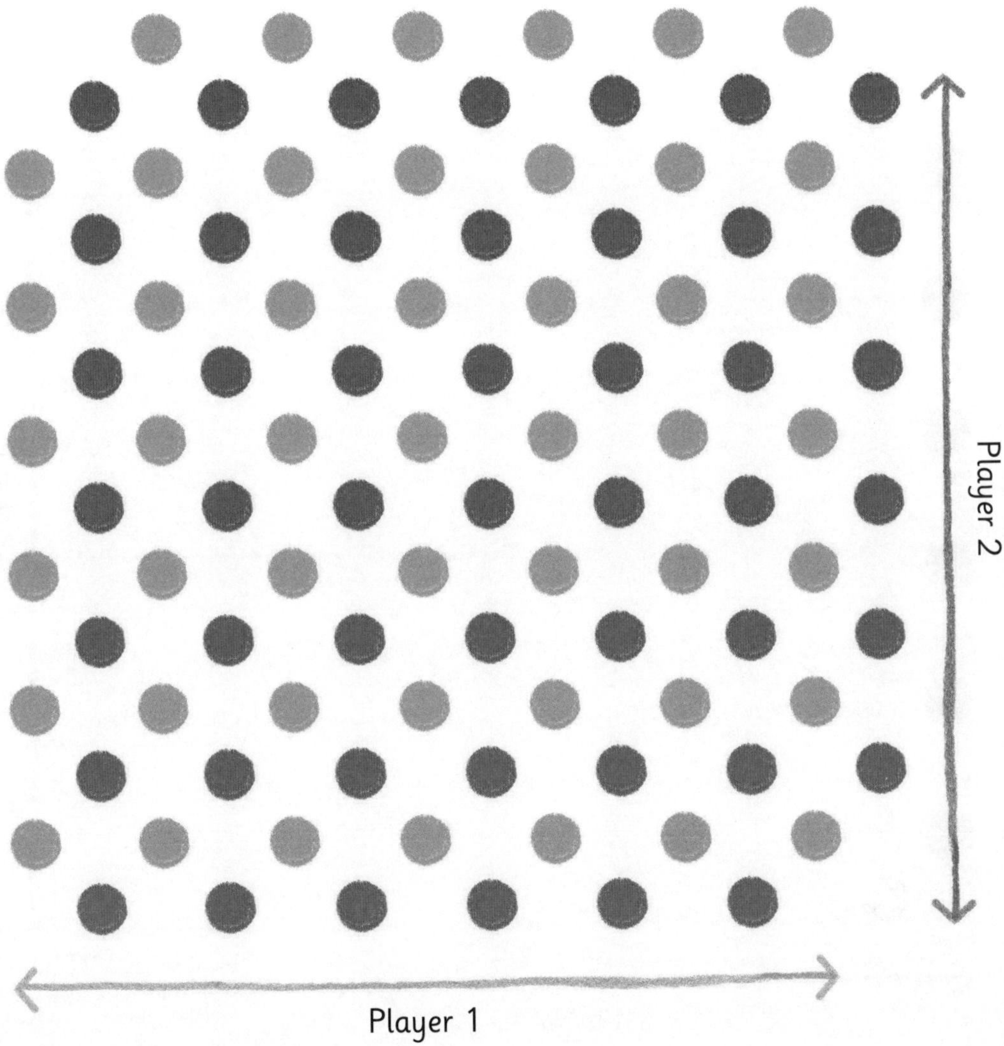

Stepping stones

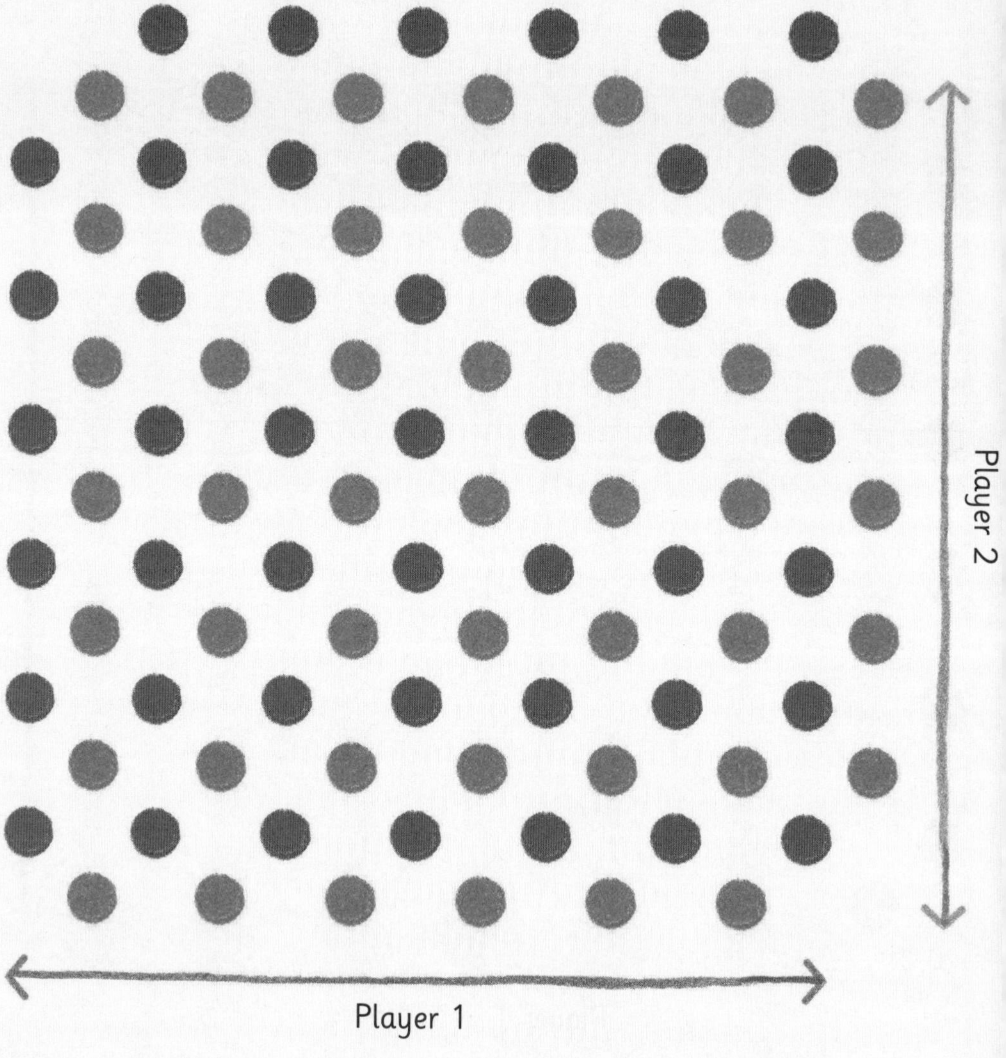

Stepping stones

20

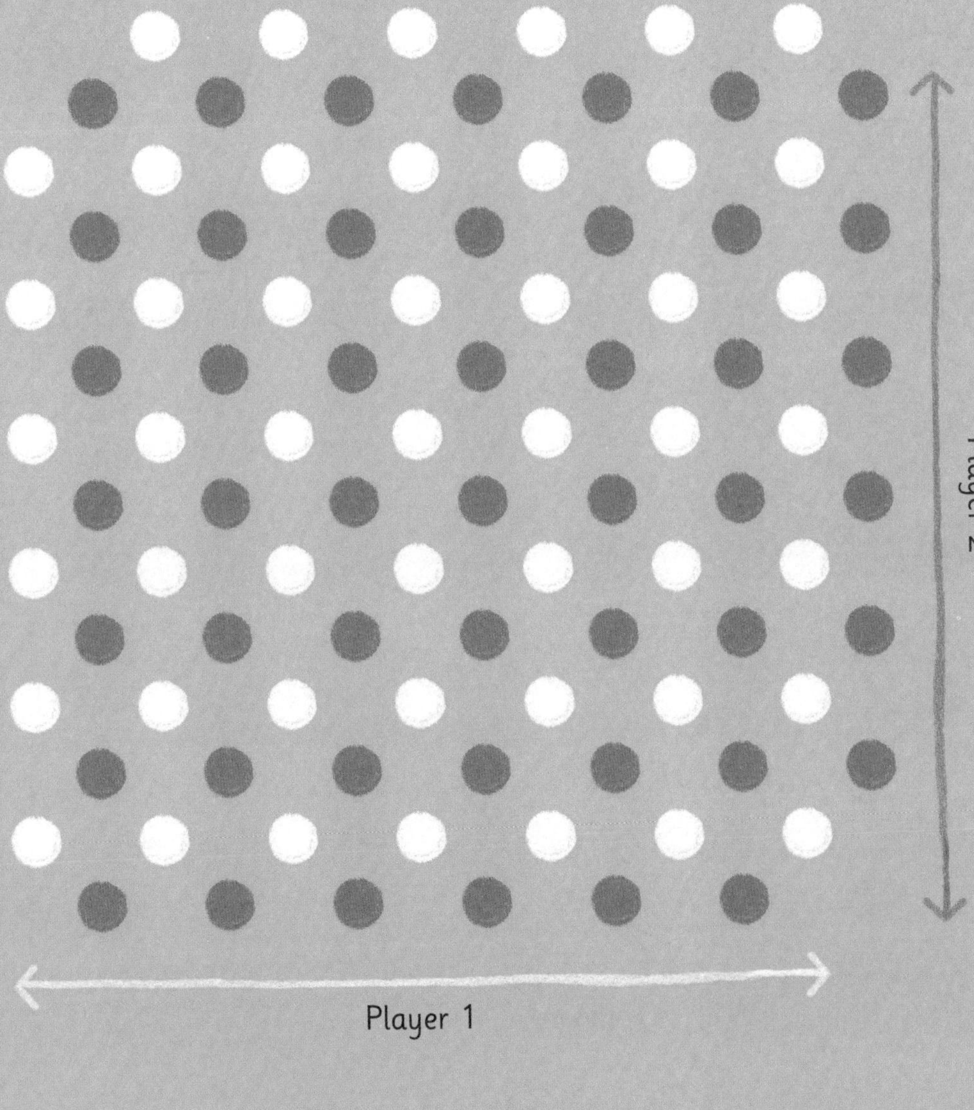

Stepping stones

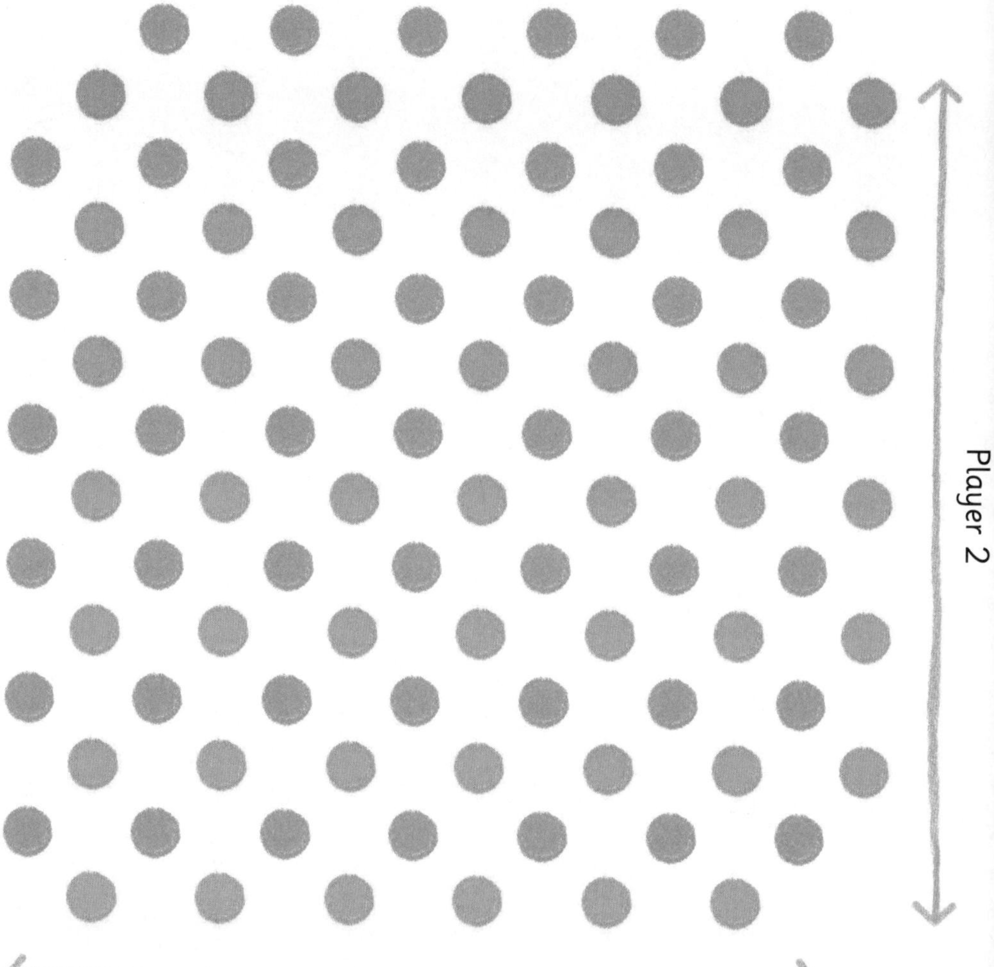

Stepping stones

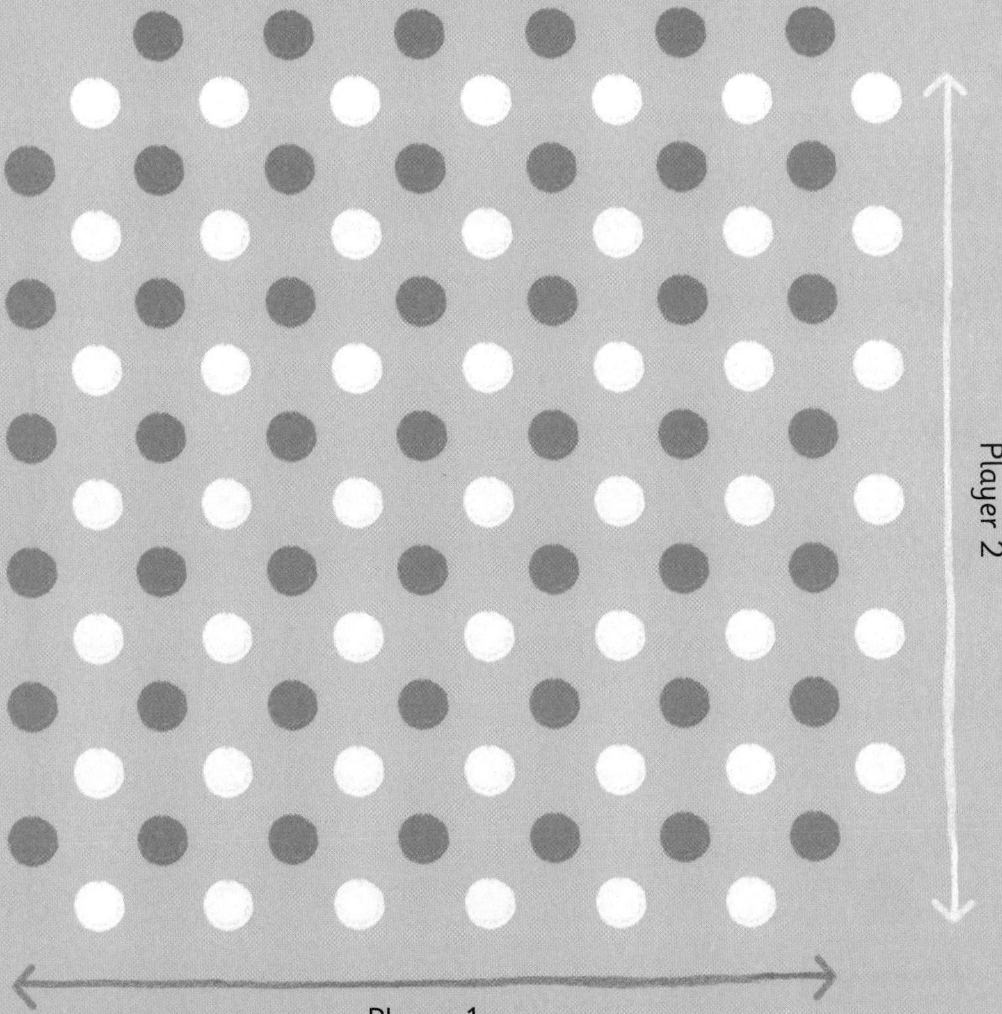

Stepping stones

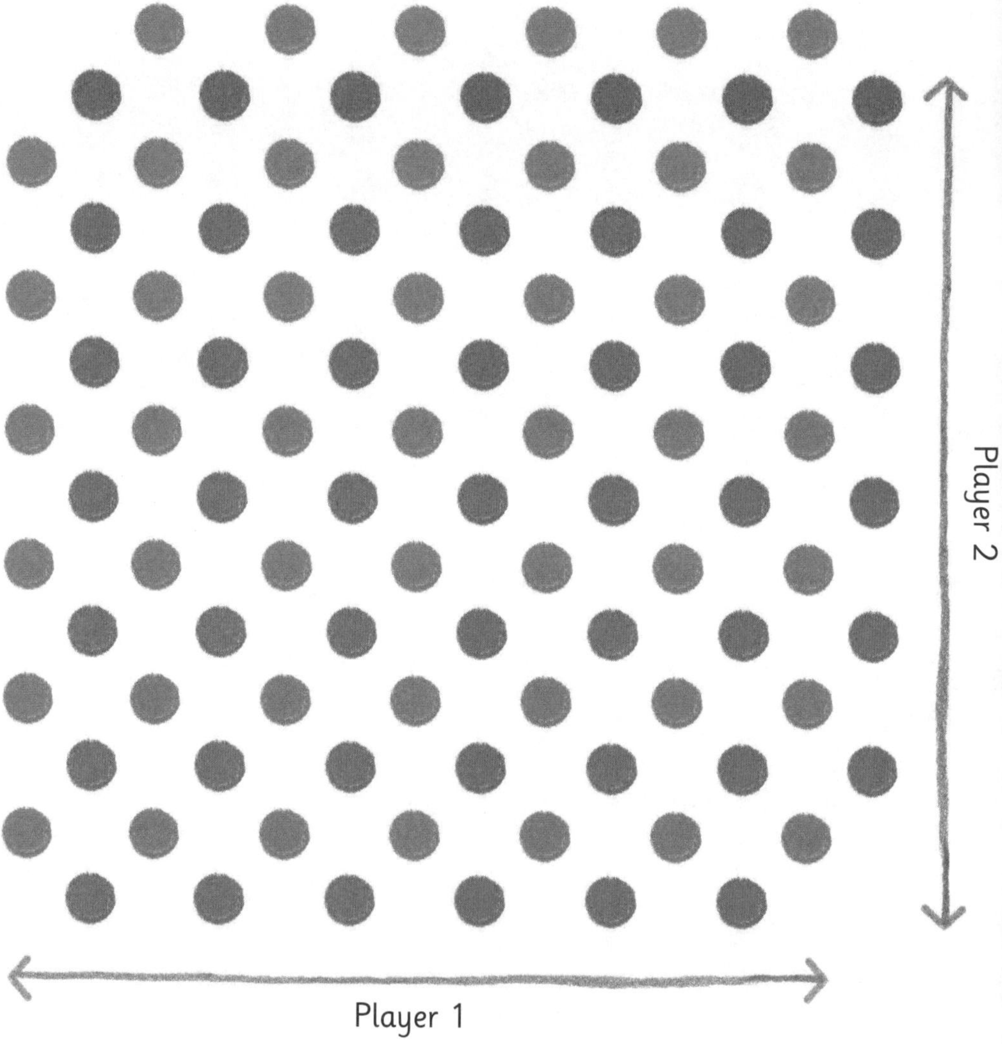

Four in a row instructions

24

1 Player 1 starts by drawing an X in any box on the bottom row.

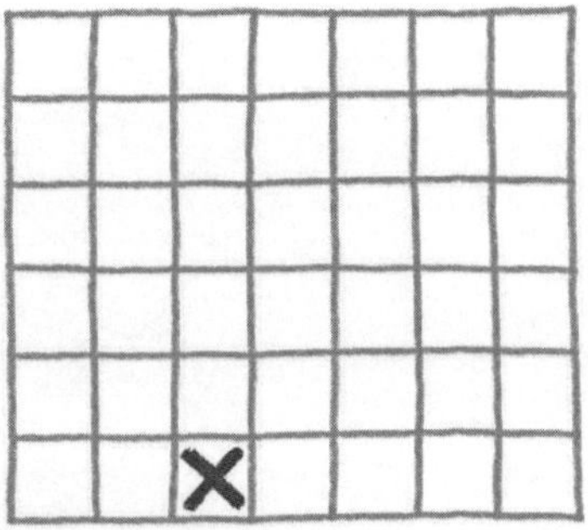

2 Player 2 then draws an O in any of the other squares on the bottom row, or in the square above the X.

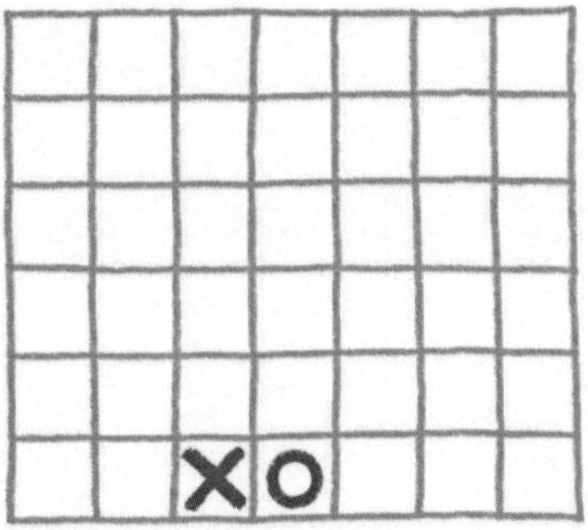

3 You can draw your symbol in any column you like, but you must always draw it in the column's lowest empty square.

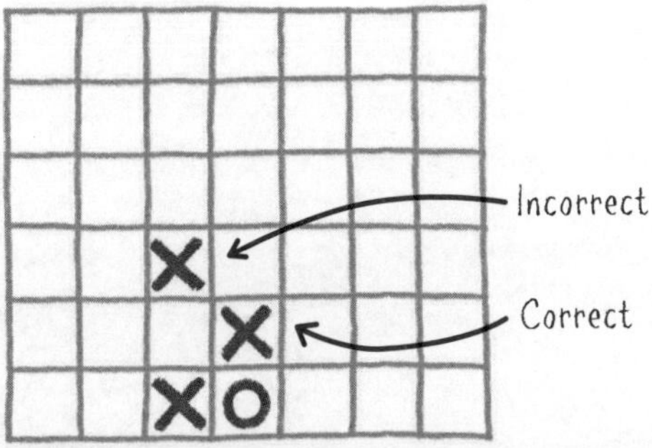

4 The first player to make a straight line of four is the winner. The line can be horizontal, vertical or diagonal. Player 1 won this game.

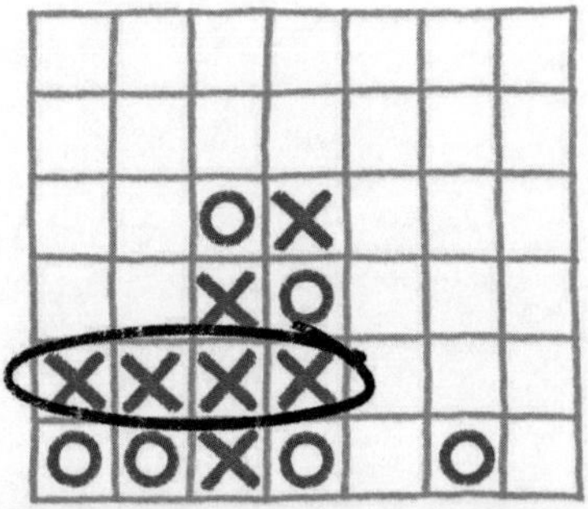

Four in a row

Four in a row

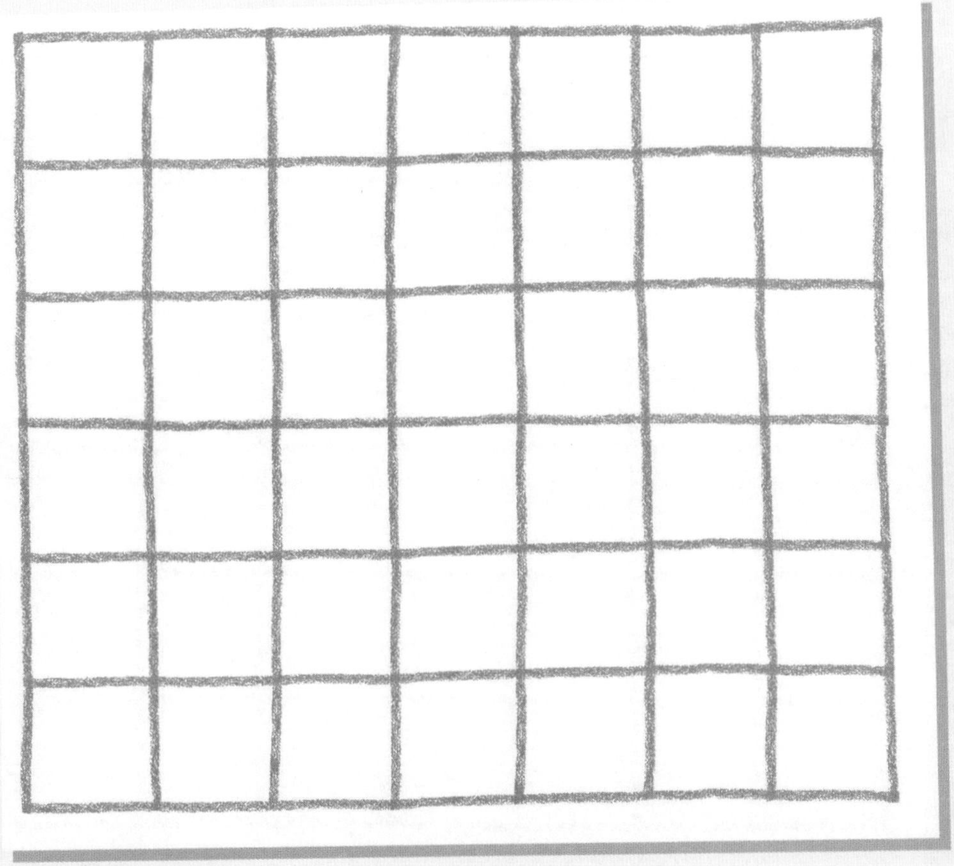

Four in a row

27

Four in a row

Four in a row

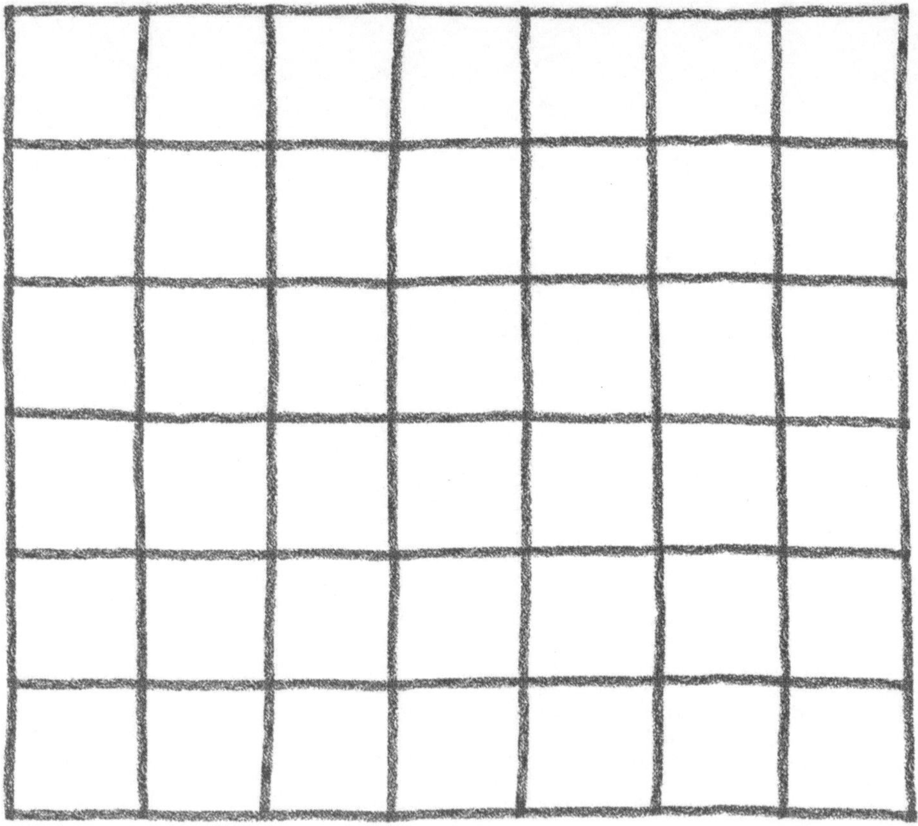

Four in a row

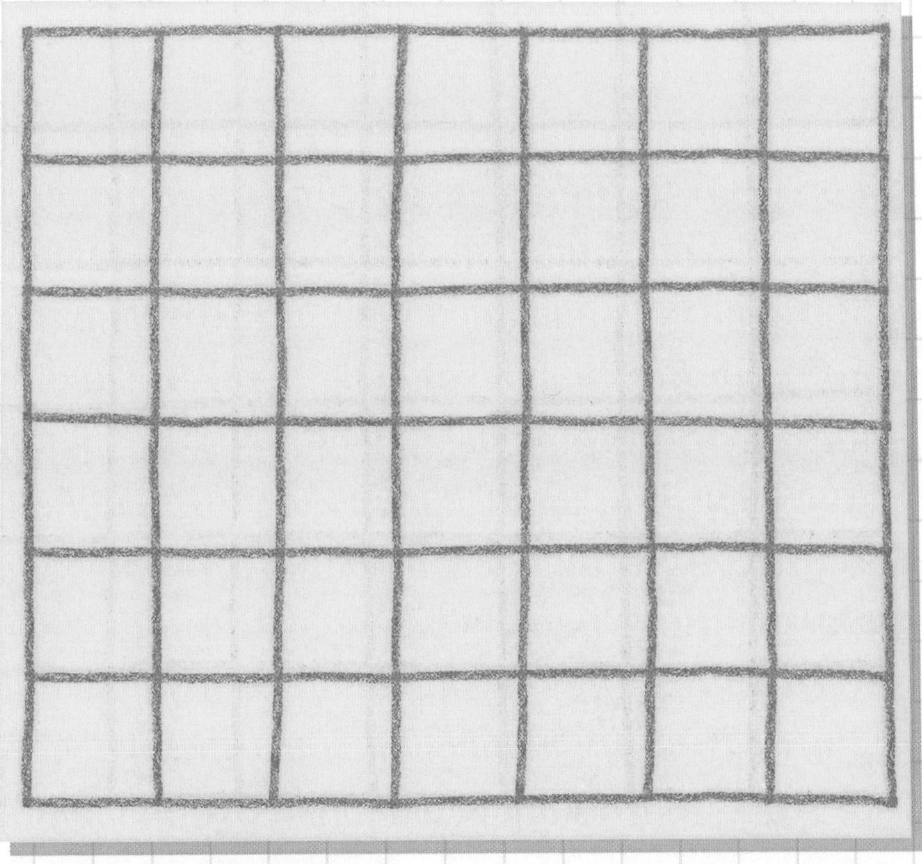

Four in a row

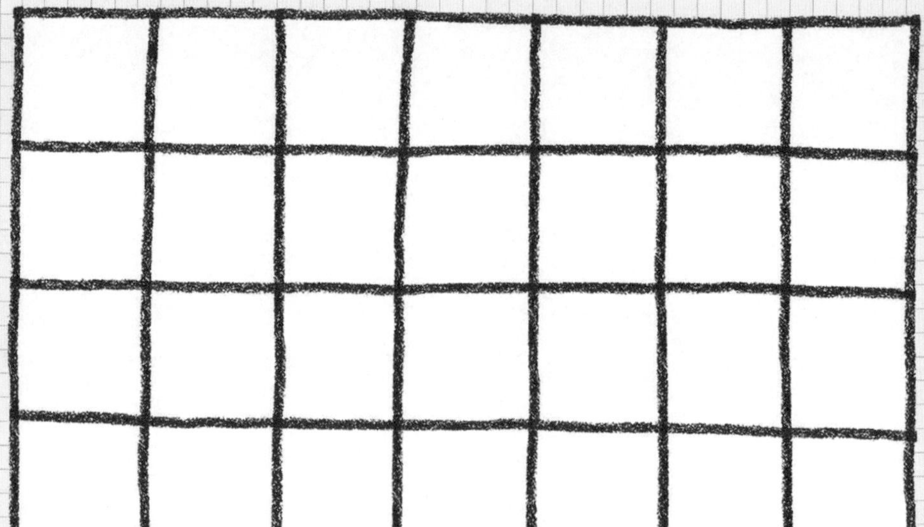

Four in a row

Four in a row

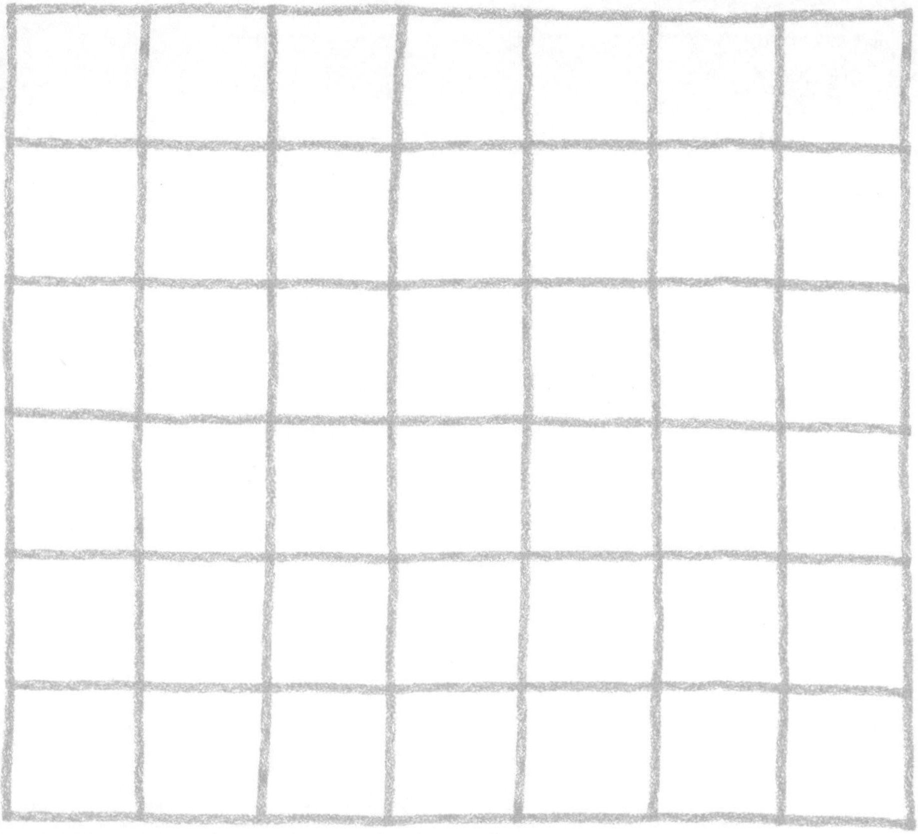

Four in a row

34

Four in a row

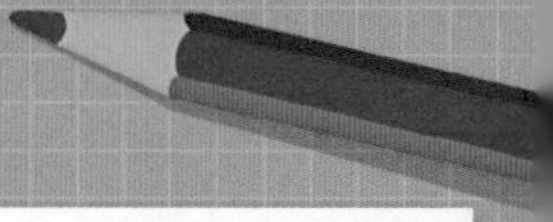

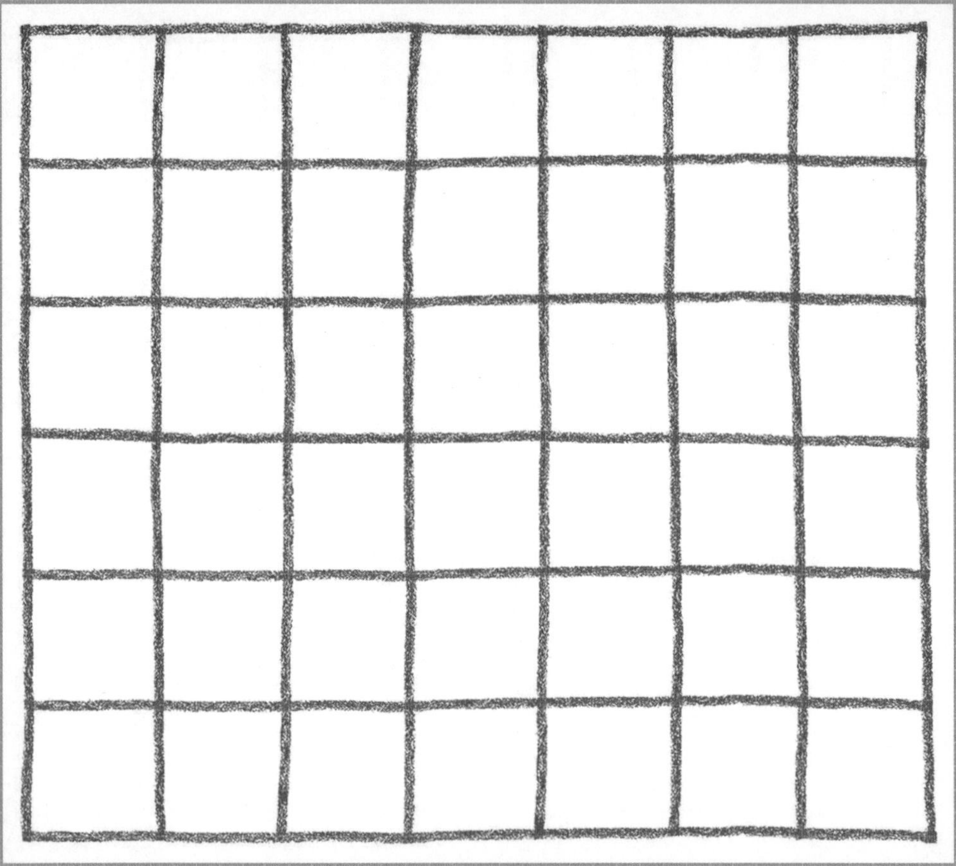

Minefield instructions

Before you begin, cut or tear along the dotted line so that each player has their own pair of grids.

1. Each player draws ten mines on the crosspoints of their minefield, and keeps them hidden from the other player. You can't have more than two mines on the same horizontal or vertical line.

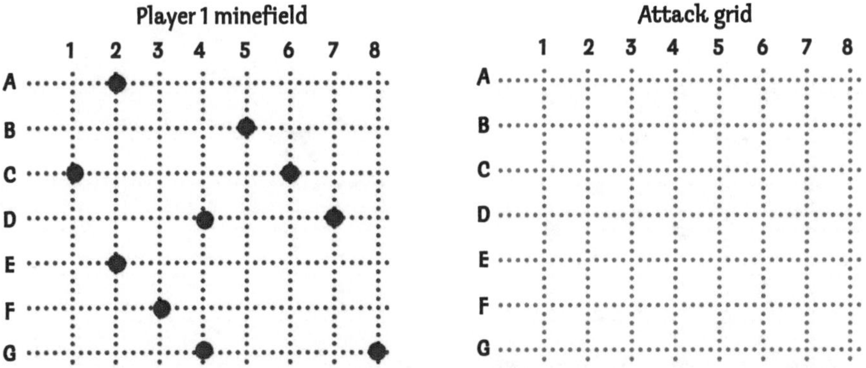

2. The aim is to move from left to right across your opponent's minefield. Starting anywhere on line 1, take turns calling out your moves. Mark your own moves on your attack grid, and your opponent's moves on your minefield.

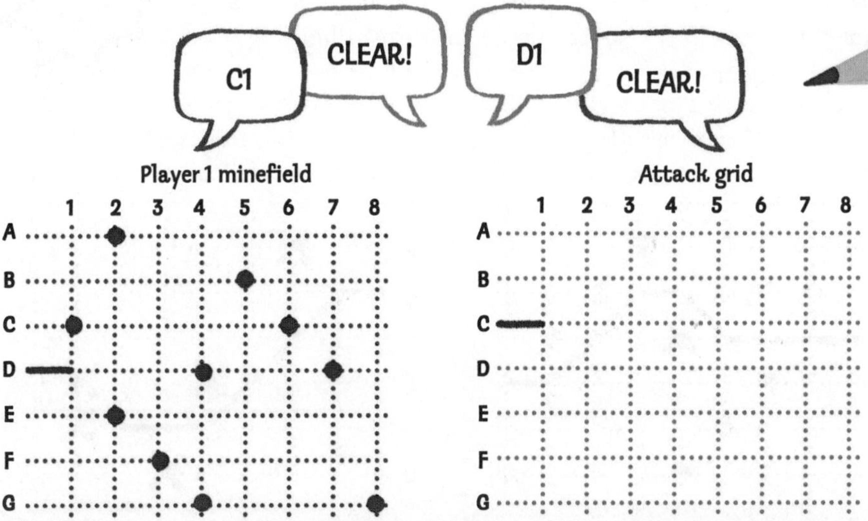

3 You can move one square at a time, either vertically, horizontally or diagonally. If you find a mine, don't move onto it, but mark it on your grid. On your next turn, find a route around the mine.

Player 1 minefield

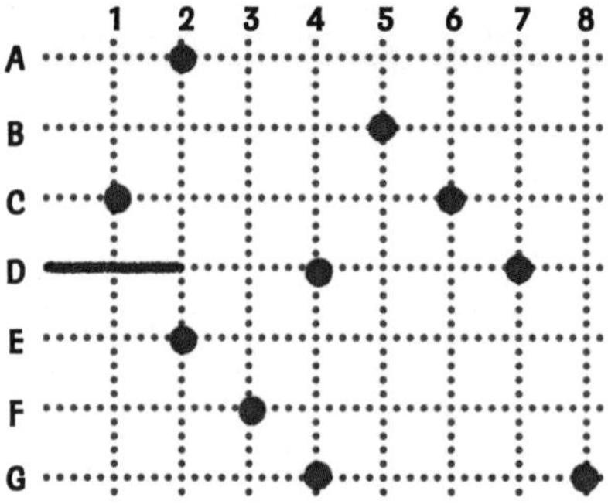

Attack grid

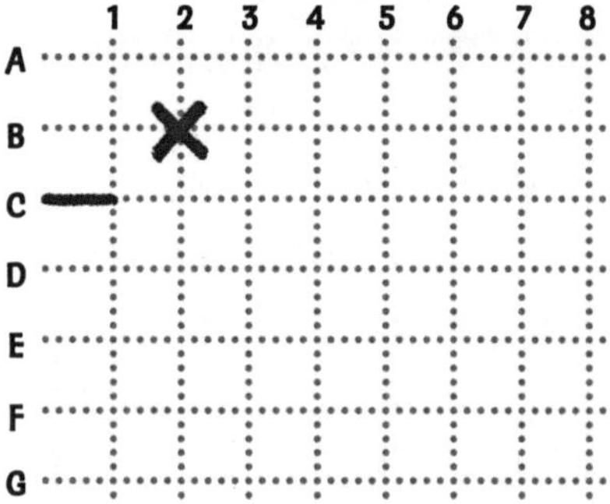

4 The first player to make it safely to the right side of the grid is the winner. The game is a tie if both players make it across in the same number of turns. Player 2 won this game.

Player 1 minefield

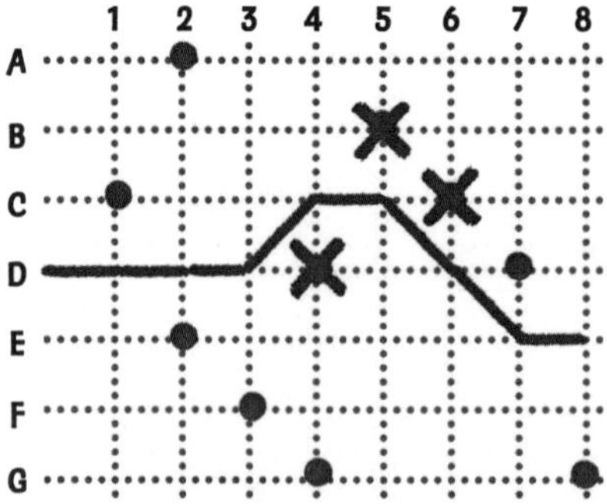

Attack grid

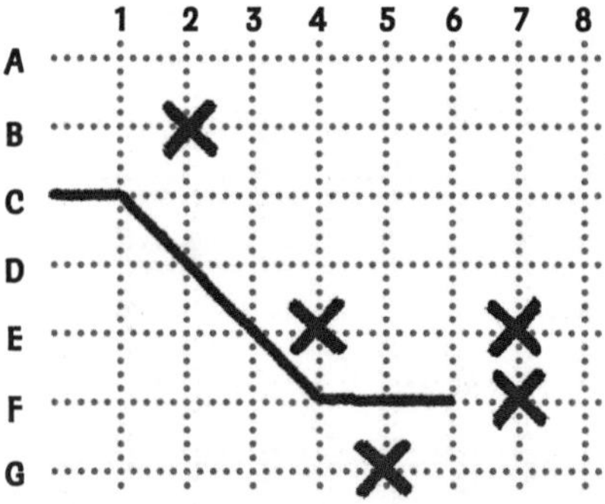

Minefield

Player 1 minefield:

	1	2	3	4	5	6	7	8
A								
B								
C								
D								
E								
F								
G								

Attack grid:

	1	2	3	4	5	6	7	8
A								
B								
C								
D								
E								
F								
G								

Cut or tear along the dotted line.

Player 2 minefield:

	1	2	3	4	5	6	7	8
A								
B								
C								
D								
E								
F								
G								

Attack grid:

	1	2	3	4	5	6	7	8
A								
B								
C								
D								
E								
F								
G								

Minefield

Player 1 minefield:

	1	2	3	4	5	6	7	8
A								
B								
C								
D								
E								
F								
G								

Attack grid:

BOOM!

	1	2	3	4	5	6	7	8
A								
B								
C								
D								
E								
F								
G								

Cut or tear along the dotted line.

Player 2 minefield:

	1	2	3	4	5	6	7	8
A								
B								
C								
D								
E								
F								
G								

Attack grid:

	1	2	3	4	5	6	7	8
A								
B								
C								
D								
E								
F								
G								

Minefield

Player 1 minefield:

	1	2	3	4	5	6	7	8
A								
B								
C								
D								
E								
F								
G								

Attack grid:

	1	2	3	4	5	6	7	8
A								
B								
C								
D								
E								
F								
G								

Cut or tear along the dotted line.

Player 2 minefield:

	1	2	3	4	5	6	7	8
A								
B								
C								
D								
E								
F								
G								

Attack grid:

	1	2	3	4	5	6	7	8
A								
B								
C								
D								
E								
F								
G								

Minefield

Player 1 minefield:

	1	2	3	4	5	6	7	8
A								
B								
C								
D								
E								
F								
G								

Attack grid:

	1	2	3	4	5	6	7	8
A								
B								
C								
D								
E								
F								
G								

Cut or tear along the dotted line.

Player 2 minefield:

	1	2	3	4	5	6	7	8
A								
B								
C								
D								
E								
F								
G								

Attack grid:

	1	2	3	4	5	6	7	8
A								
B								
C								
D								
E								
F								
G								

Minefield

Player 1 minefield:

	1	2	3	4	5	6	7	8
A								
B								
C								
D								
E								
F								
G								

Attack grid:

	1	2	3	4	5	6	7	8
A								
B								
C								
D								
E								
F								
G								

Cut or tear along the dotted line.

Player 2 minefield:

	1	2	3	4	5	6	7	8
A								
B								
C								
D								
E								
F								
G								

Attack grid:

	1	2	3	4	5	6	7	8
A								
B								
C								
D								
E								
F								
G								

Minefield

Player 1 minefield:

	1	2	3	4	5	6	7	8
A								
B								
C								
D								
E								
F								
G								

Attack grid:

	1	2	3	4	5	6	7	8
A								
B								
C								
D								
E								
F								
G								

Cut or tear along the dotted line.

Player 2 minefield:

	1	2	3	4	5	6	7	8
A								
B								
C								
D								
E								
F								
G								

Attack grid:

	1	2	3	4	5	6	7	8
A								
B								
C								
D								
E								
F								
G								

Minefield

Player 1 minefield:

	1	2	3	4	5	6	7	8
A								
B								
C								
D								
E								
F								
G								

Attack grid:

	1	2	3	4	5	6	7	8
A								
B								
C								
D								
E								
F								
G								

Cut or tear along the dotted line.

Player 2 minefield:

	1	2	3	4	5	6	7	8
A								
B								
C								
D								
E								
F								
G								

Attack grid:

	1	2	3	4	5	6	7	8
A								
B								
C								
D								
E								
F								
G								

Minefield

Player 1 minefield:

	1	2	3	4	5	6	7	8
A								
B								
C								
D								
E								
F								
G								

Attack grid:

	1	2	3	4	5	6	7	8
A								
B								
C								
D								
E								
F								
G								

Cut or tear along the dotted line.

Player 2 minefield:

	1	2	3	4	5	6	7	8
A								
B								
C								
D								
E								
F								
G								

Attack grid:

	1	2	3	4	5	6	7	8
A								
B								
C								
D								
E								
F								
G								

Minefield

Player 1 minefield:

	1	2	3	4	5	6	7	8
A								
B								
C								
D								
E								
F								
G								

Attack grid:

	1	2	3	4	5	6	7	8
A								
B								
C								
D								
E								
F								
G								

Cut or tear along the dotted line.

Player 2 minefield:

	1	2	3	4	5	6	7	8
A								
B								
C								
D								
E								
F								
G								

Attack grid:

	1	2	3	4	5	6	7	8
A								
B								
C								
D								
E								
F								
G								

Minefield

Player 1 minefield:

	1	2	3	4	5	6	7	8
A								
B								
C								
D								
E								
F								
G								

Attack grid:

	1	2	3	4	5	6	7	8
A								
B								
C								
D								
E								
F								
G								

Cut or tear along the dotted line.

Player 2 minefield:

	1	2	3	4	5	6	7	8
A								
B								
C								
D								
E								
F								
G								

Attack grid:

	1	2	3	4	5	6	7	8
A								
B								
C								
D								
E								
F								
G								

Os and Xs instructions

1 Player 1 marks an O in any of the spaces in the grid.

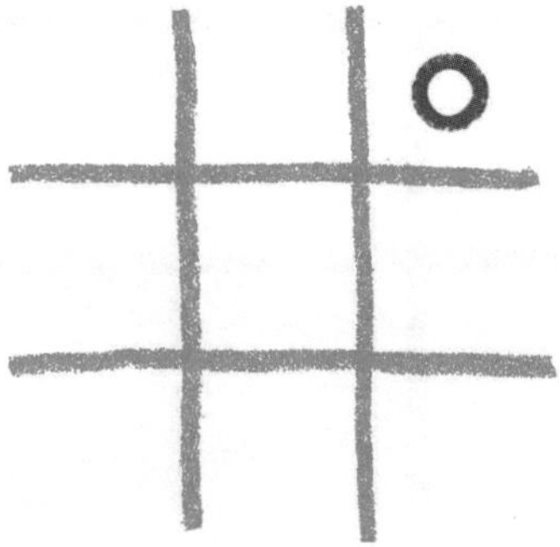

2 Player 2 marks an X in any of the other spaces.

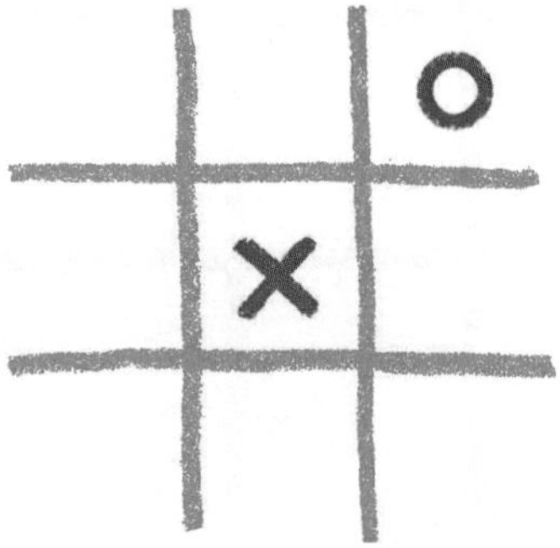

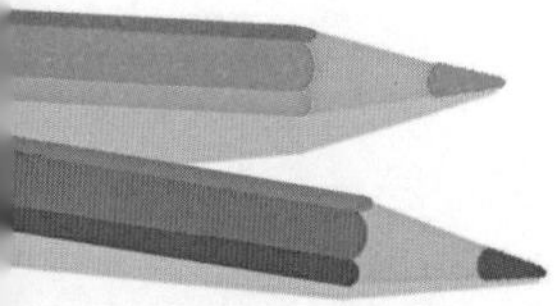

3 Taking turns, try to make a straight line of three in a row. The line can be horizontal, vertical or diagonal.

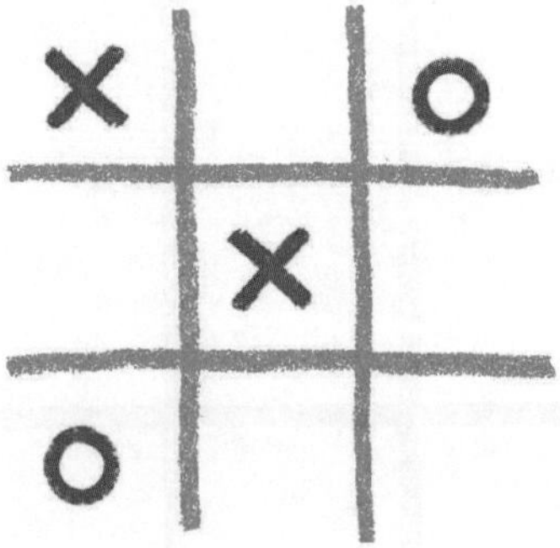

4 The winner is the first player to make a line of three in a row. If no one makes a line, the game is a tie.

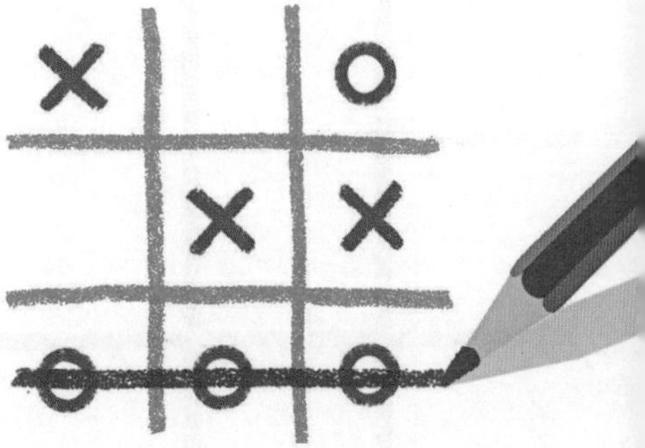

Os and Xs

48

Os and Xs

Os and Xs

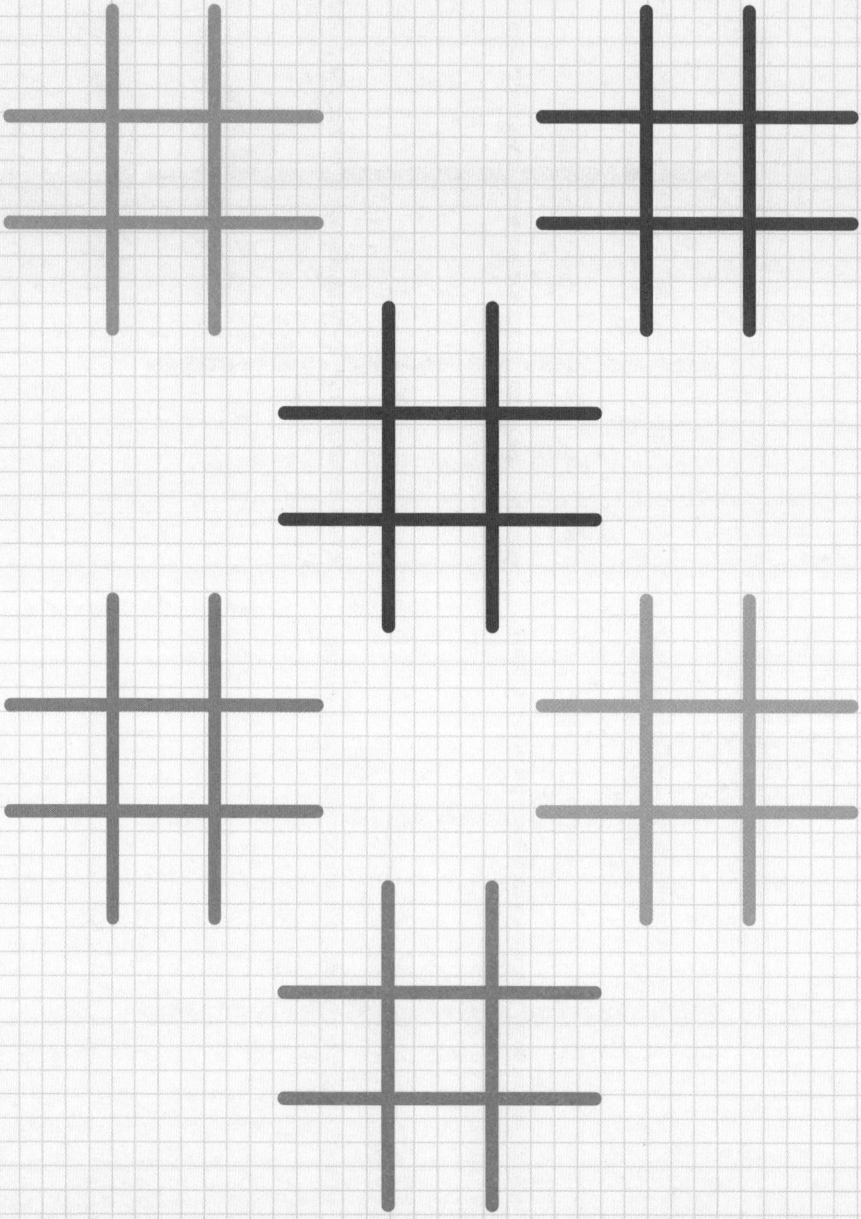

Os and Xs

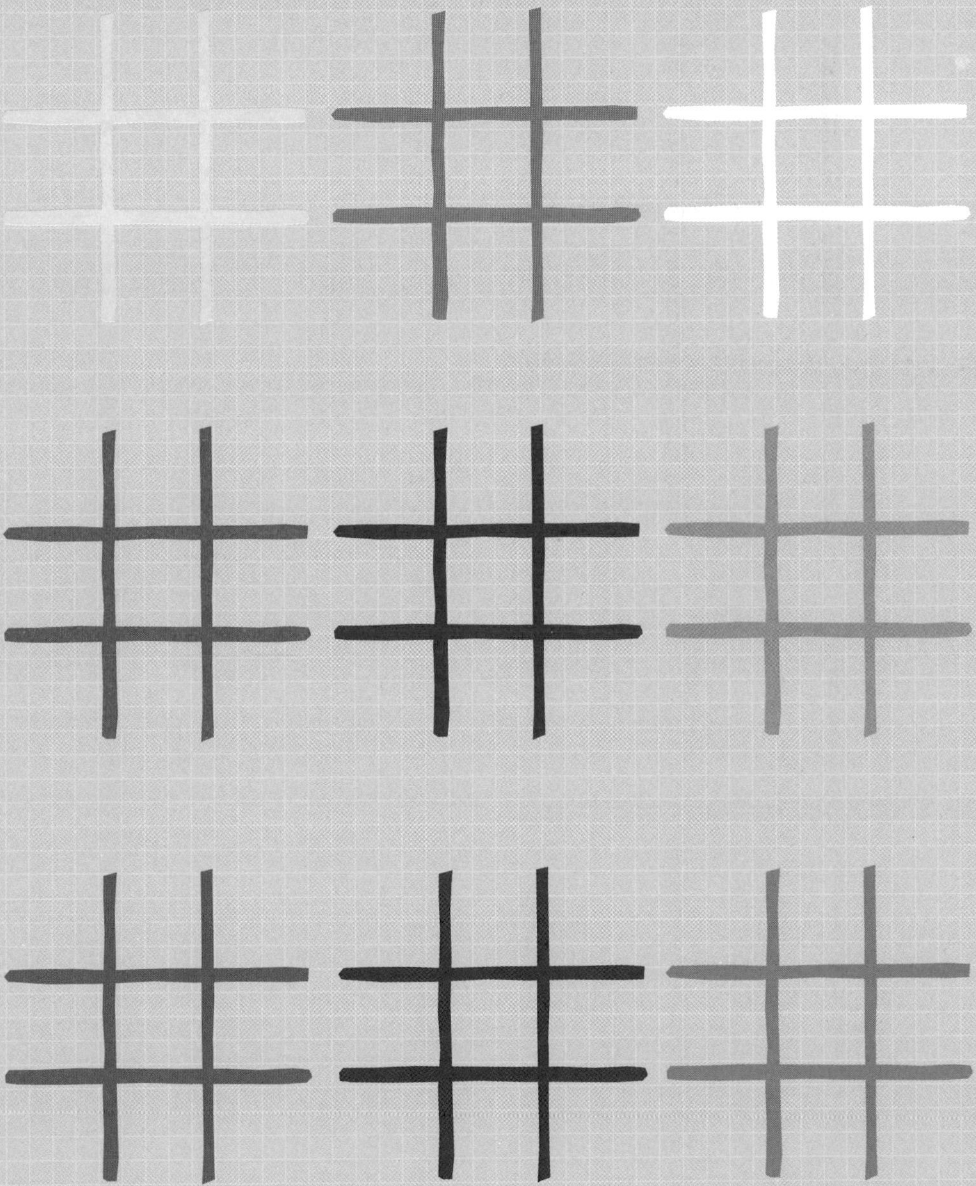

Os and Xs

52

Os and Xs

Os and Xs

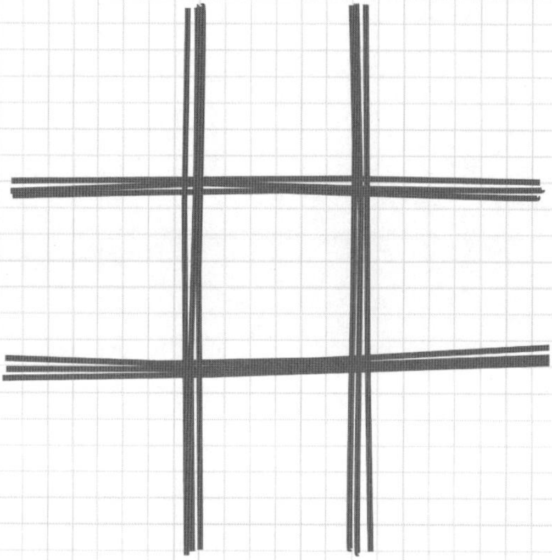

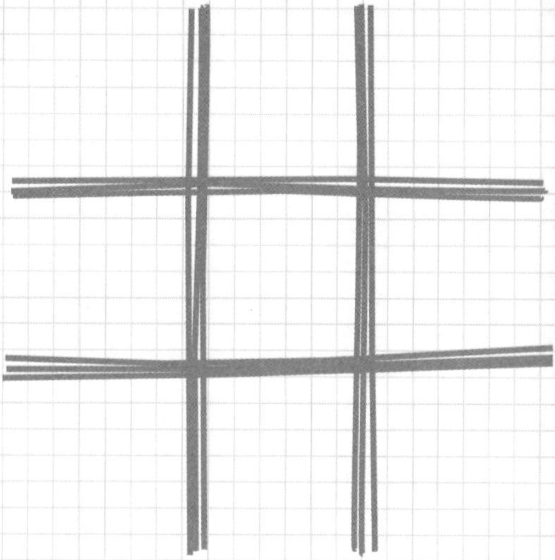

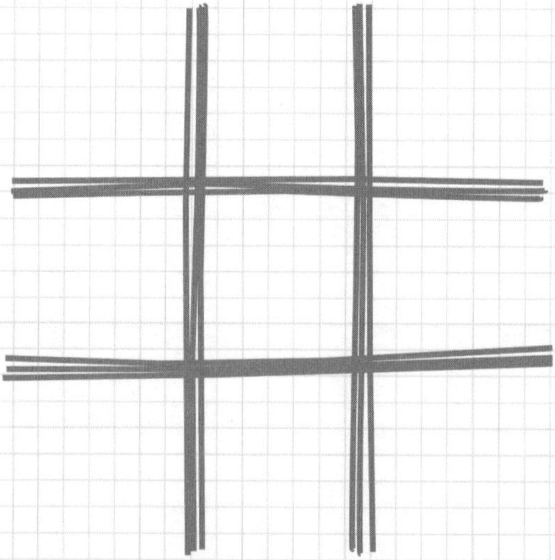

Os and Xs

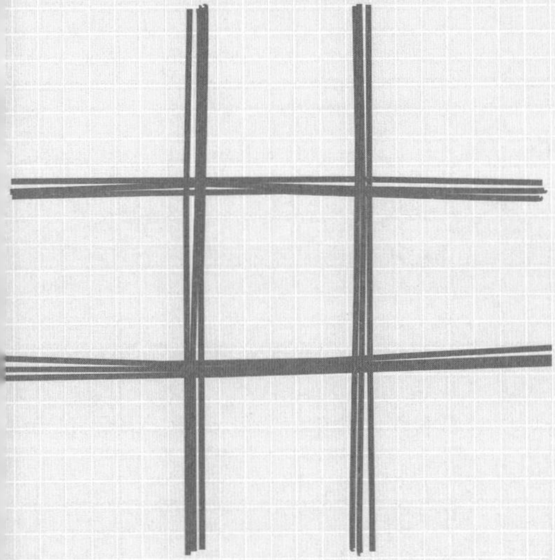

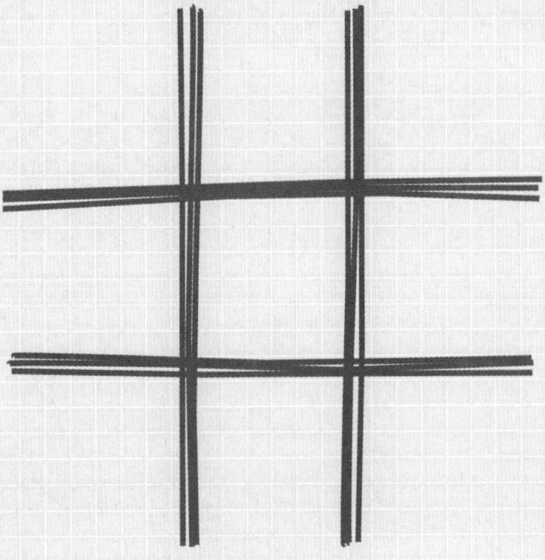

Os and Xs

Hive instructions

1 Player 1 (blue) fills in one of the hexagons on the grid.

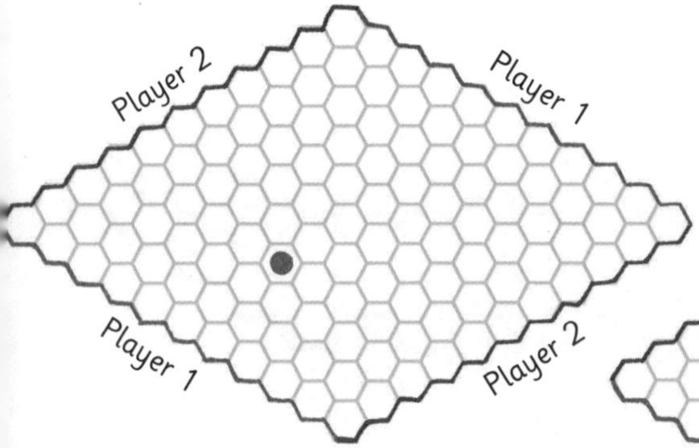

2 Player 2 (red) then fills in any of the other hexagons on the grid.

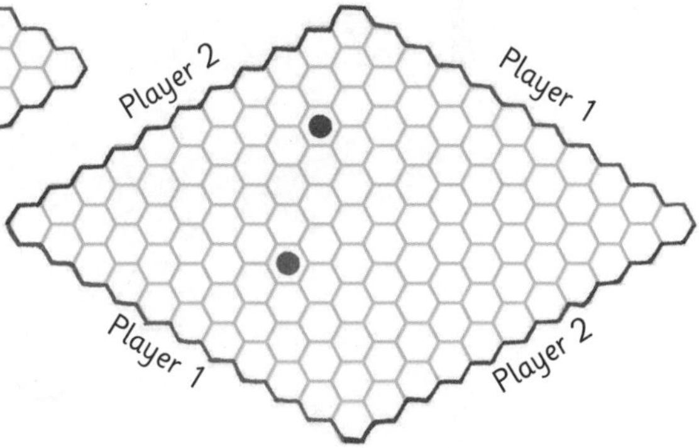

3 Taking turns, fill in hexagons anywhere on the grid. The goal is to make a chain that connects your two sides of the grid.

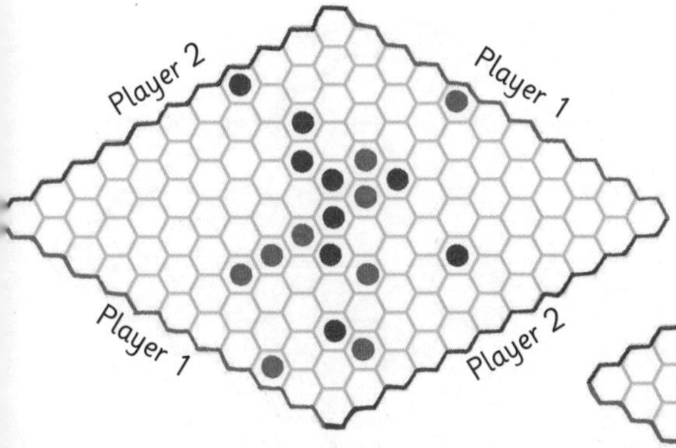

4 The winner is the first player to make a complete chain. Player 1 won this game.

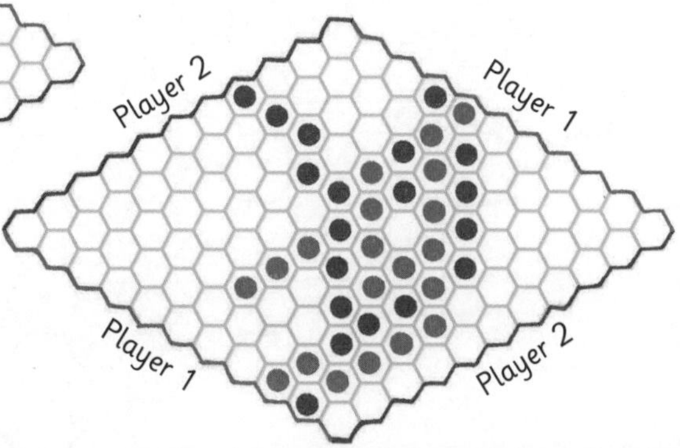

Hive

Game 1

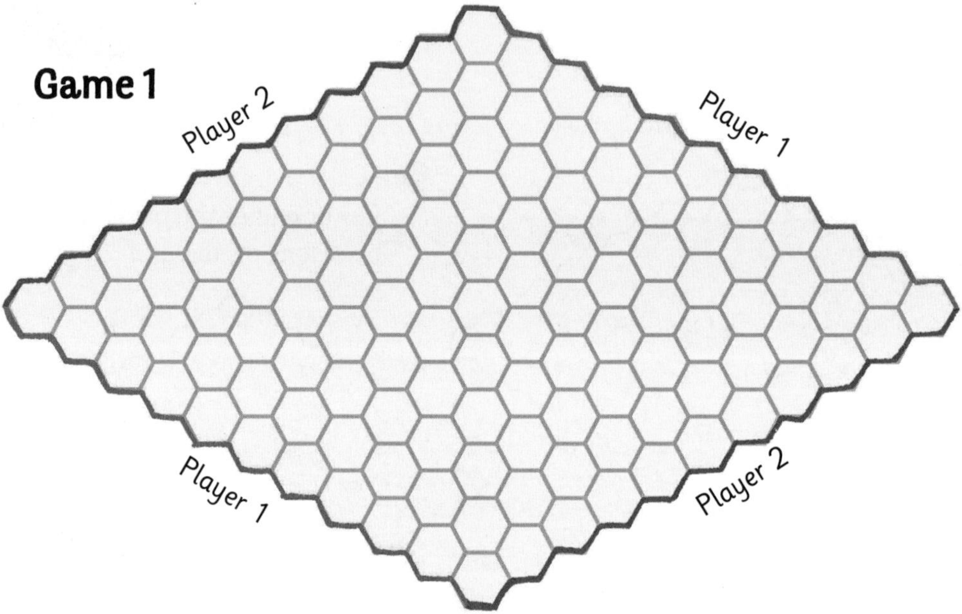

Game 2

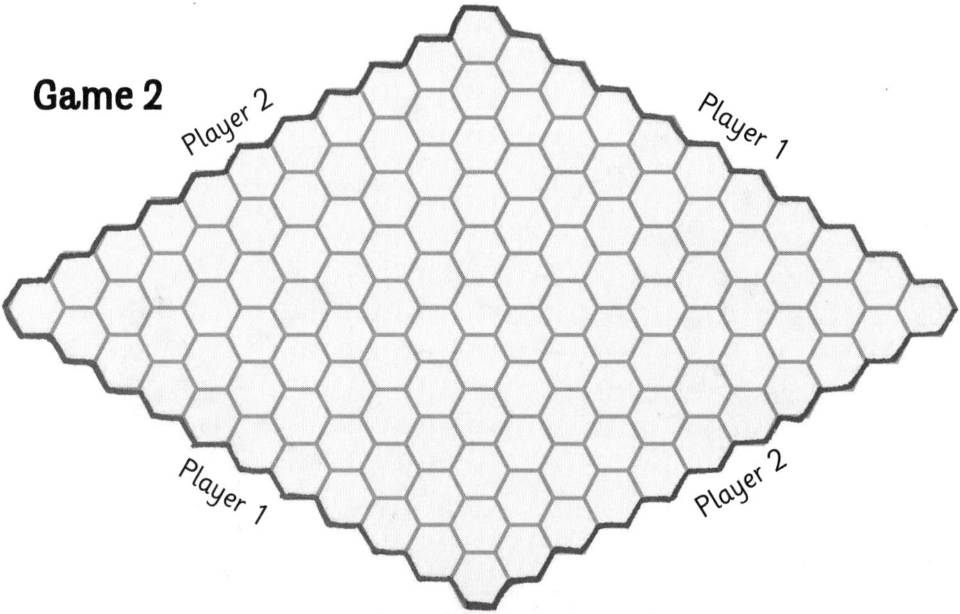

Hive

Game 1

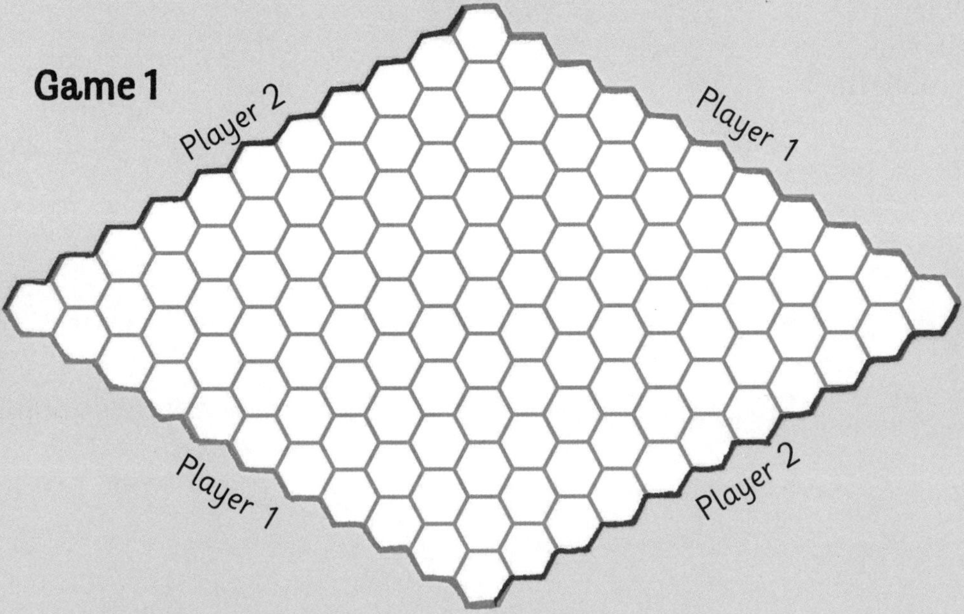

Game 2

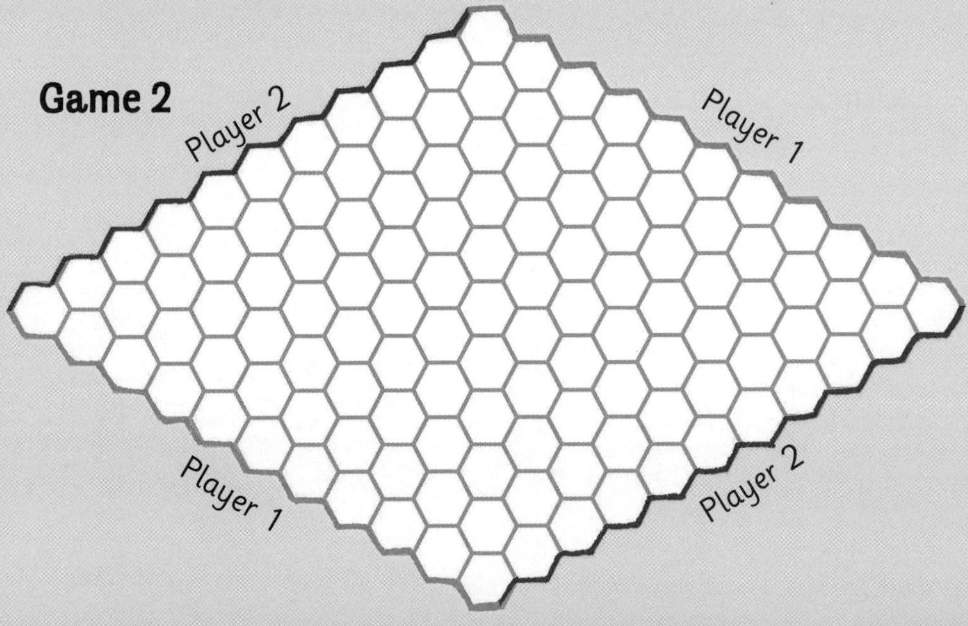

Hive

Game 1

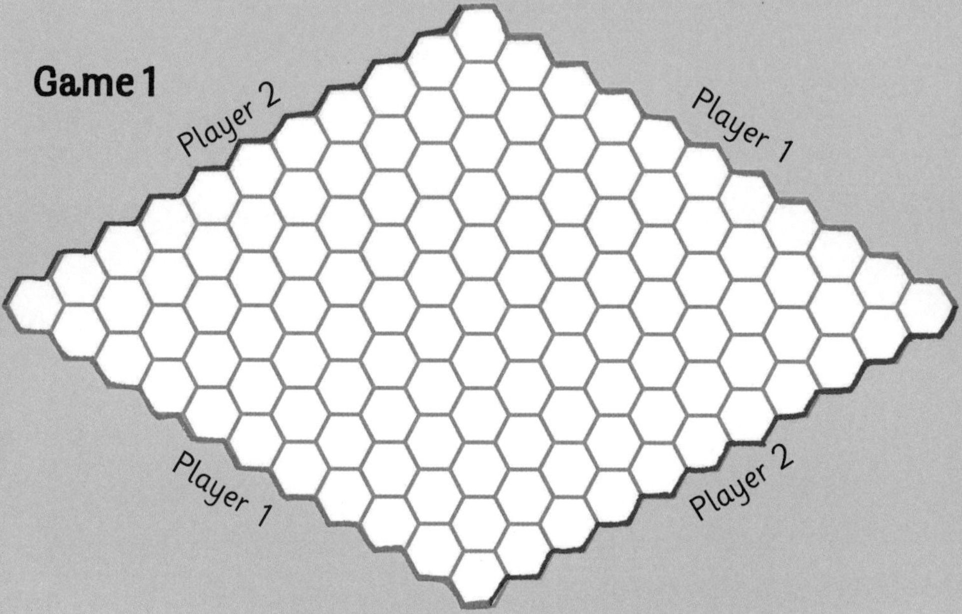

Game 2

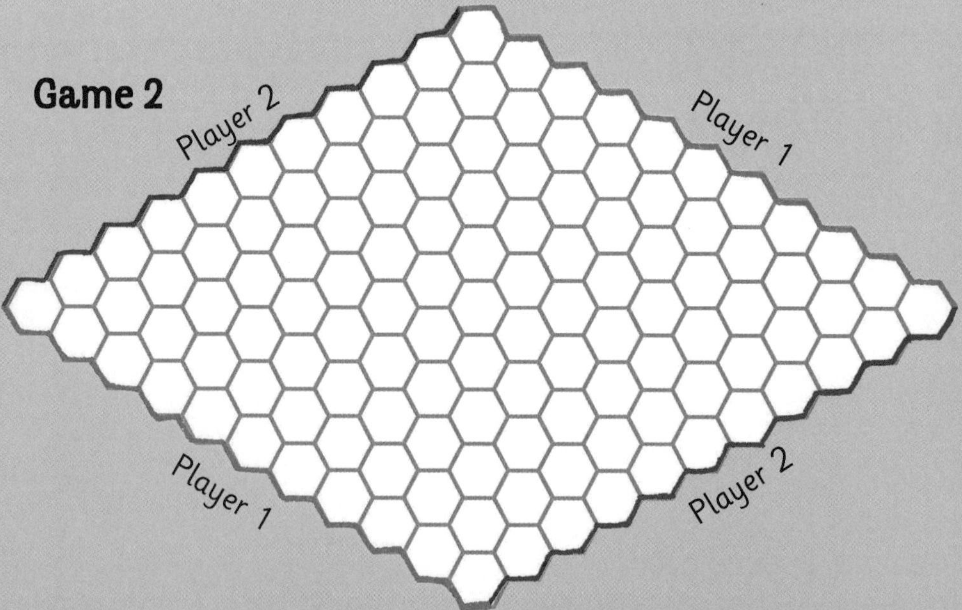

Hive

Game 1

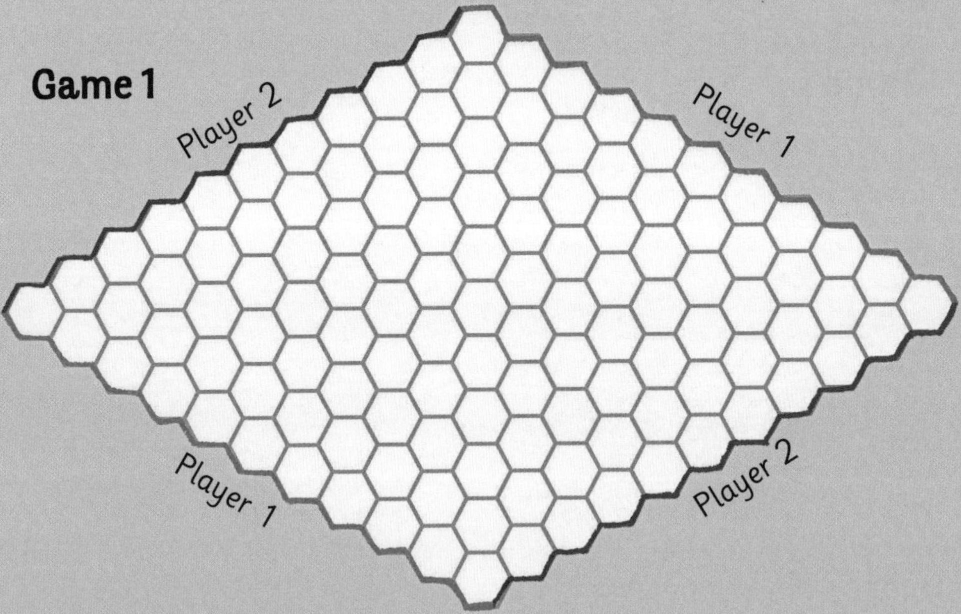

Game 2

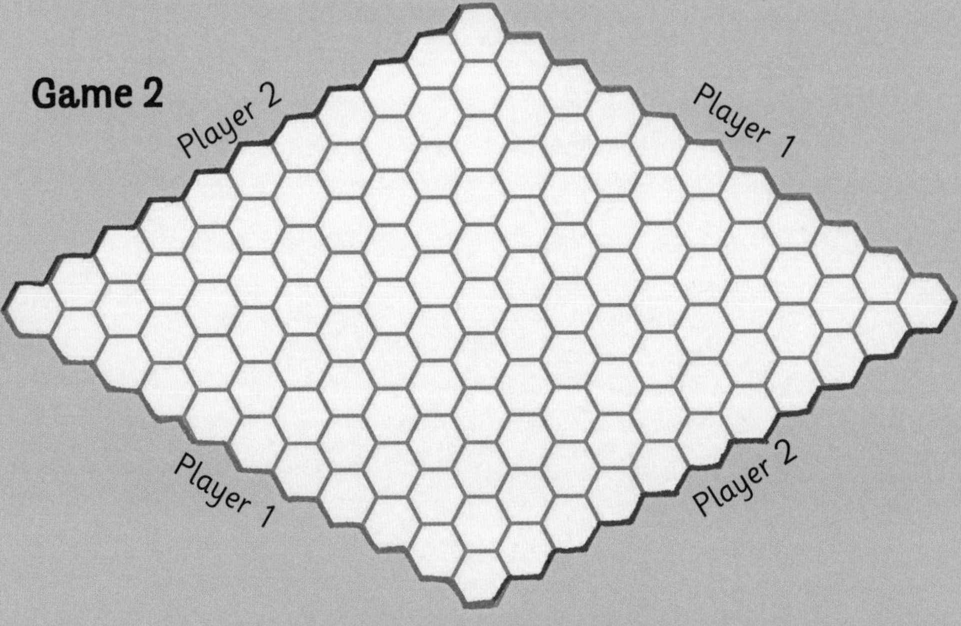

Hive

Game 1

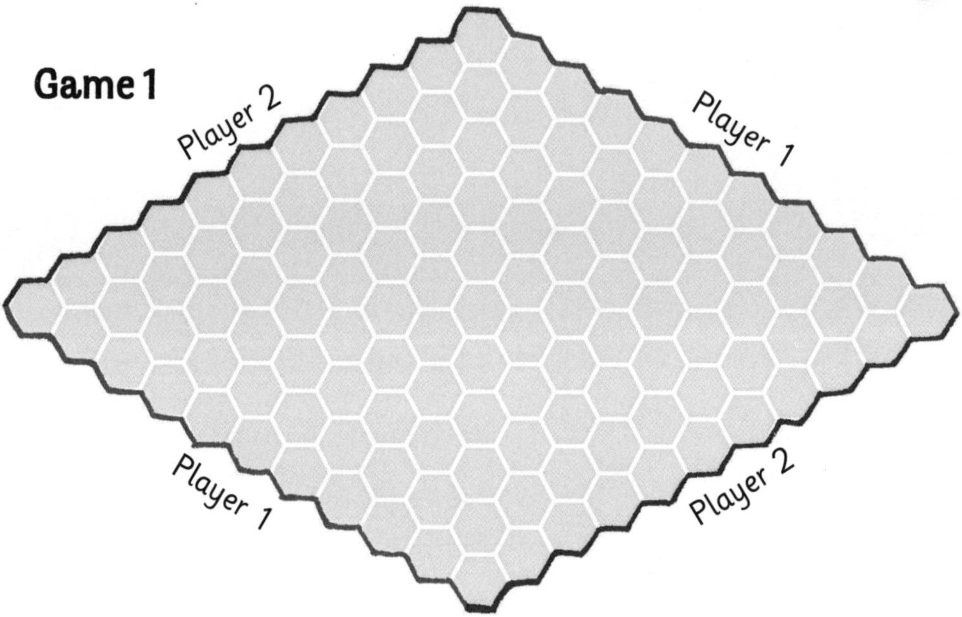

Game 2

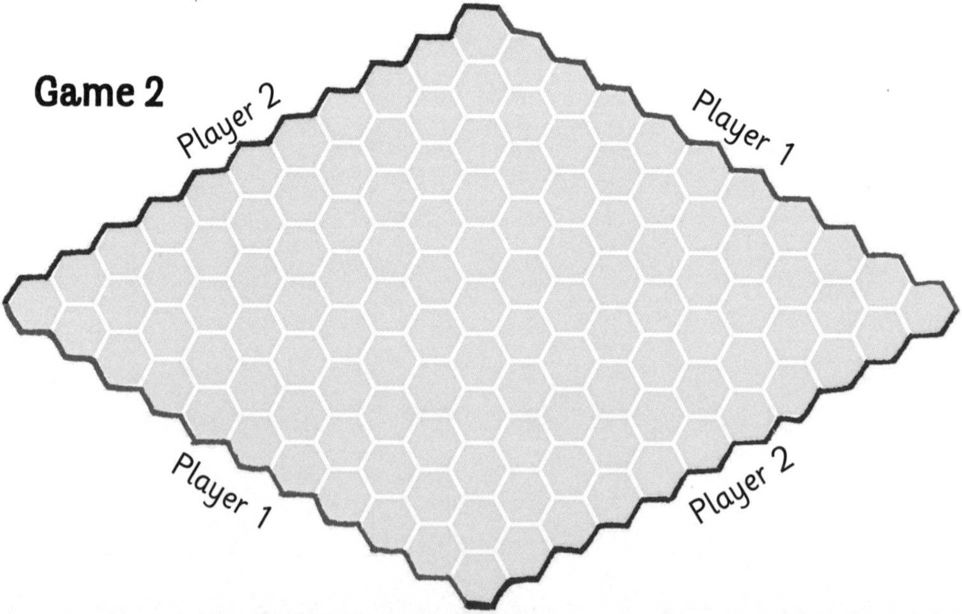

Hive

Game 1

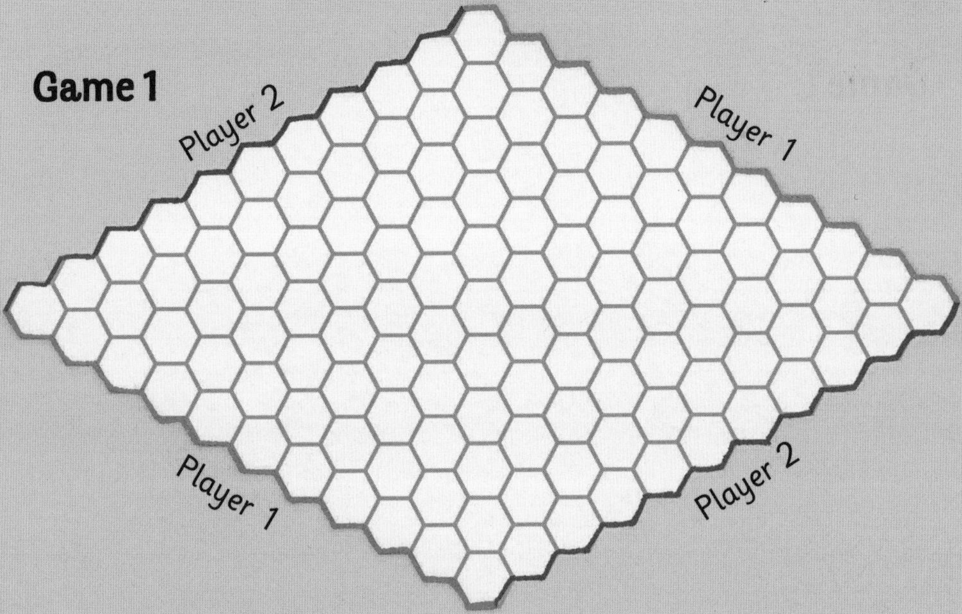

Game 2

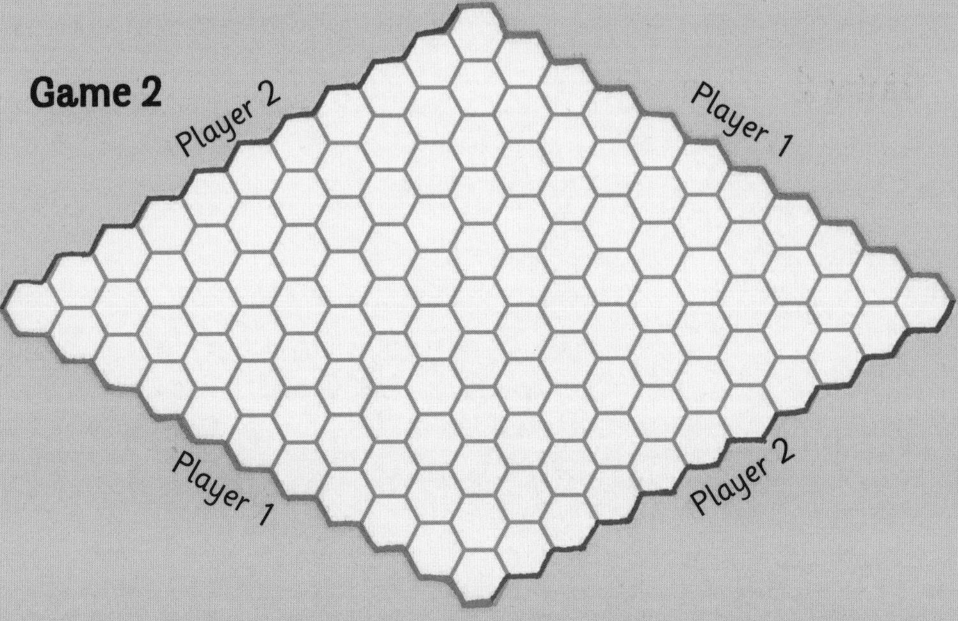

Hive

Game 1

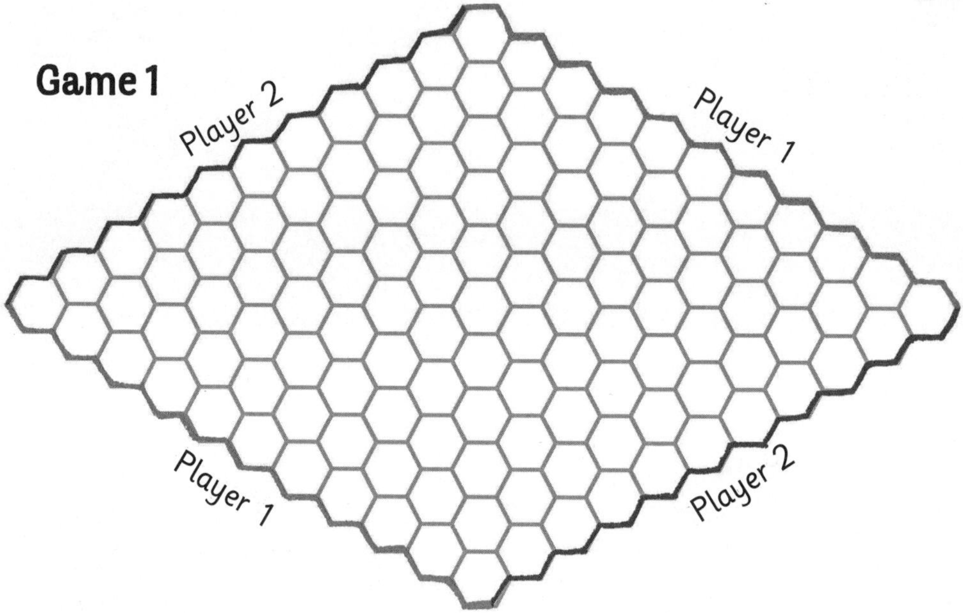

Game 2

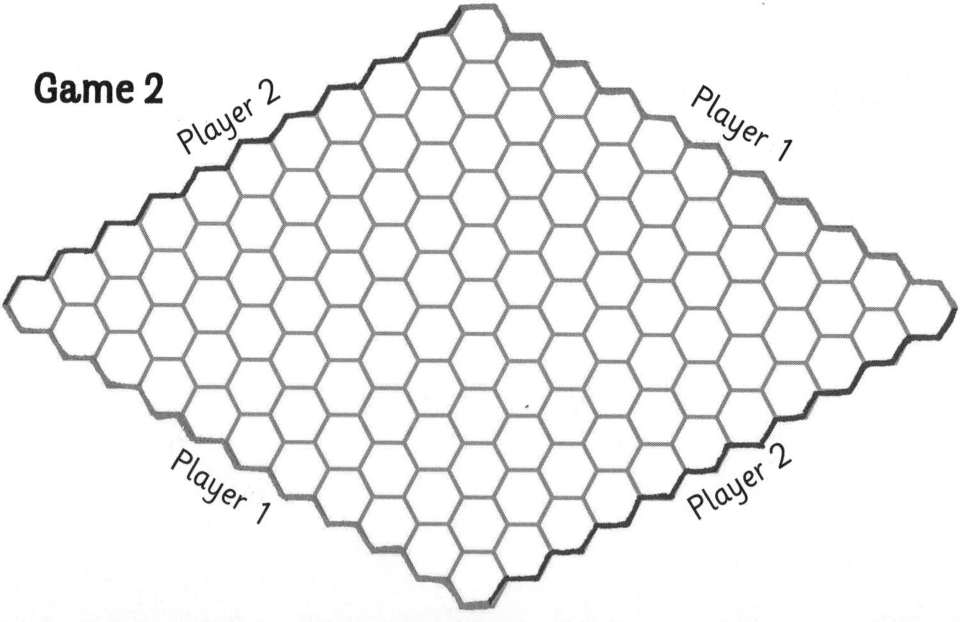

Hive

Game 1

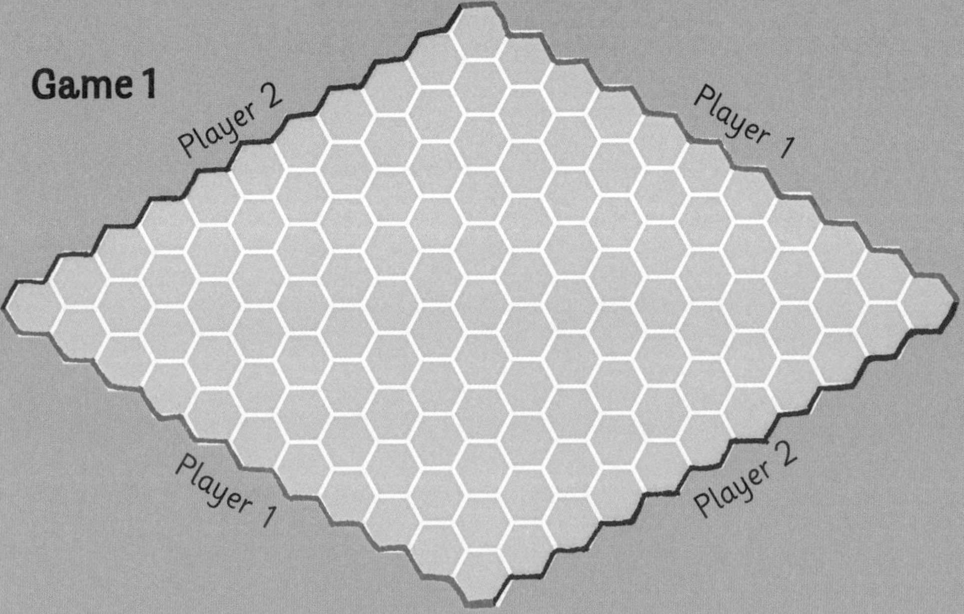

Game 2

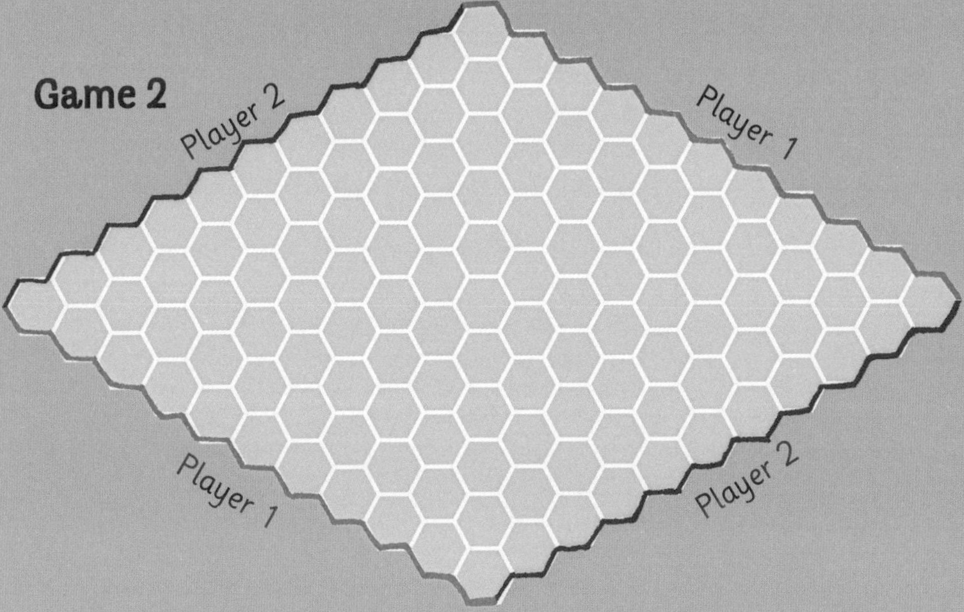

Hive

Game 1

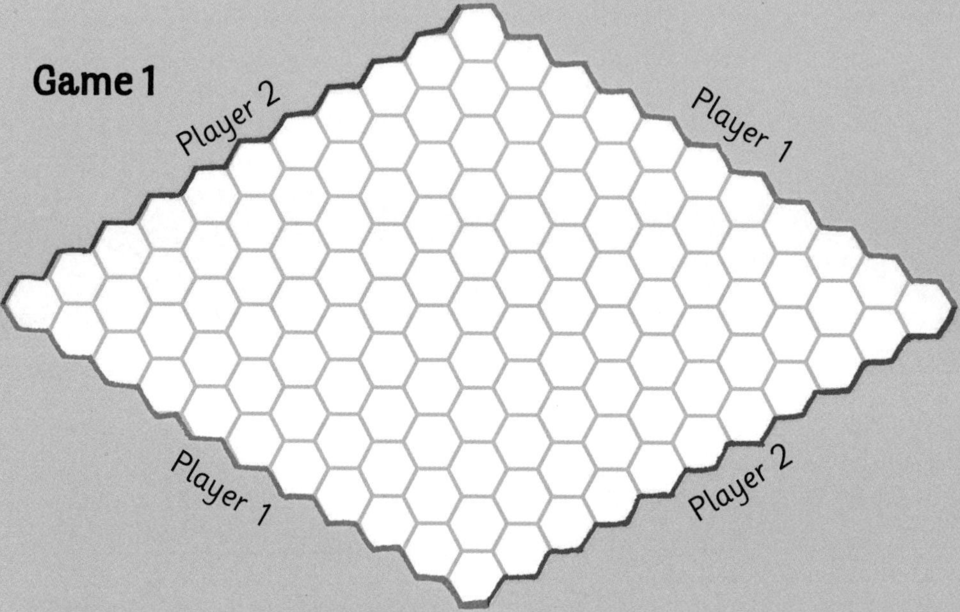

Game 2

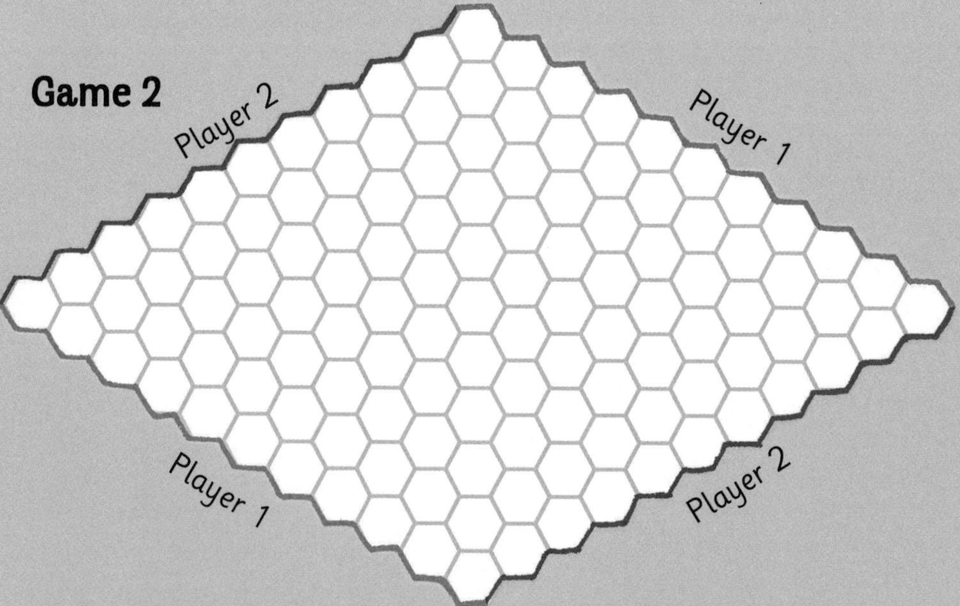

Strike out instructions

1 Player 1 (red) chooses a row, and crosses out some of its lines. You can cross out as many lines as you want, but only from that row.

2 Player 2 (blue) then chooses a row and crosses out some of its lines. You can choose the same row as Player 1, or a different row.

3 The winner is the player who crosses out the last line.

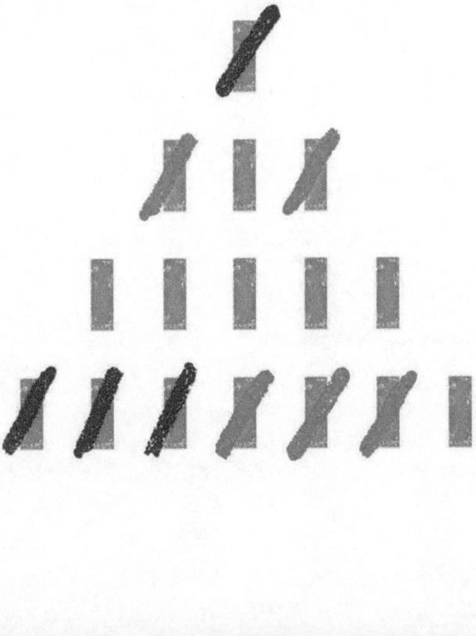

4 Player 2 won this game.

Strike out

68

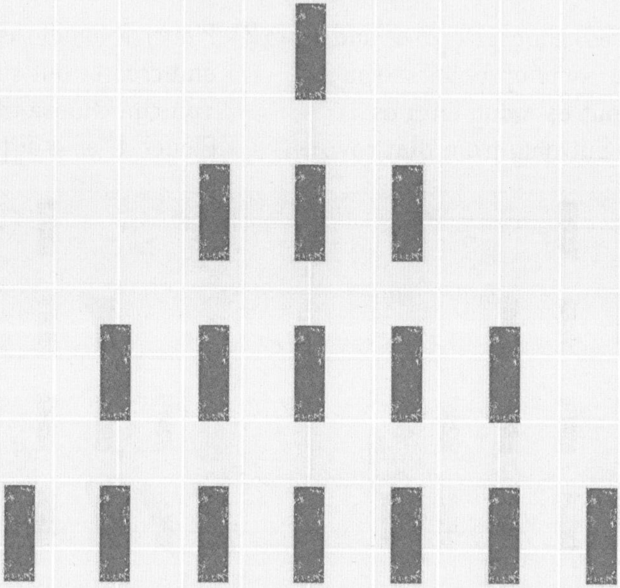

Game 1

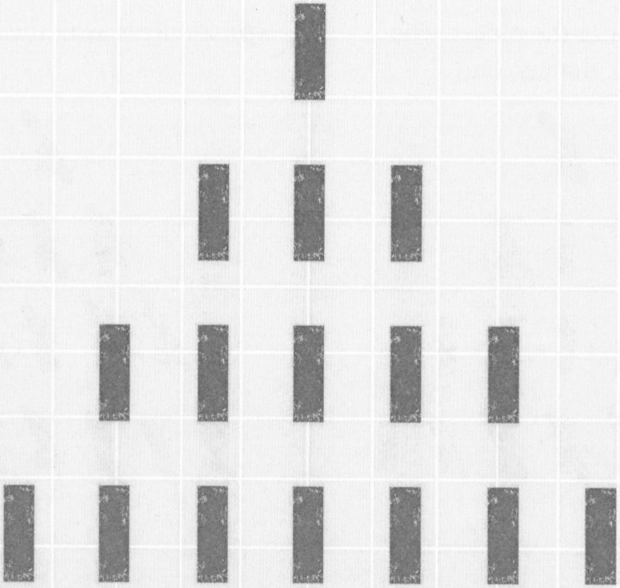

Game 2

Strike out

Game 1

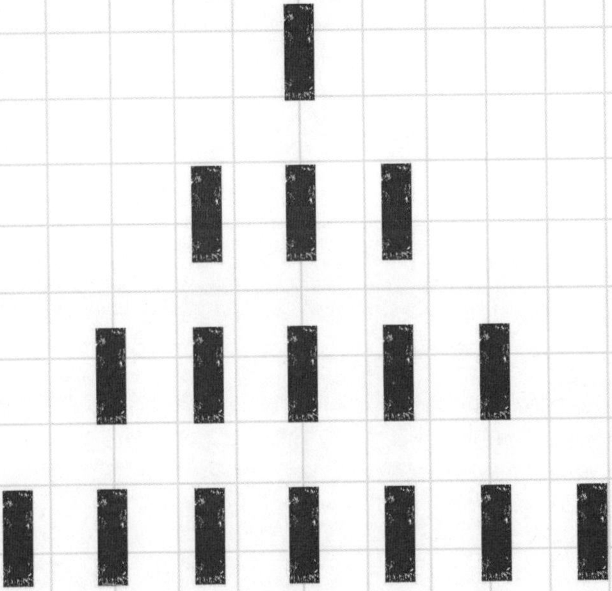

Game 2

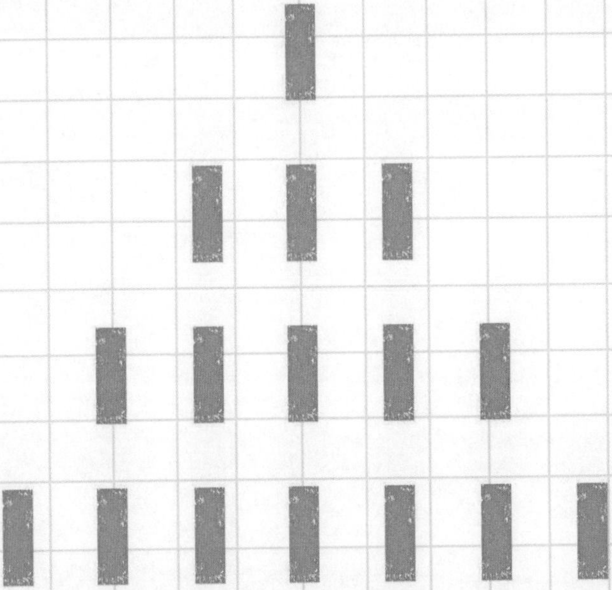

Strike out

70

Game 1

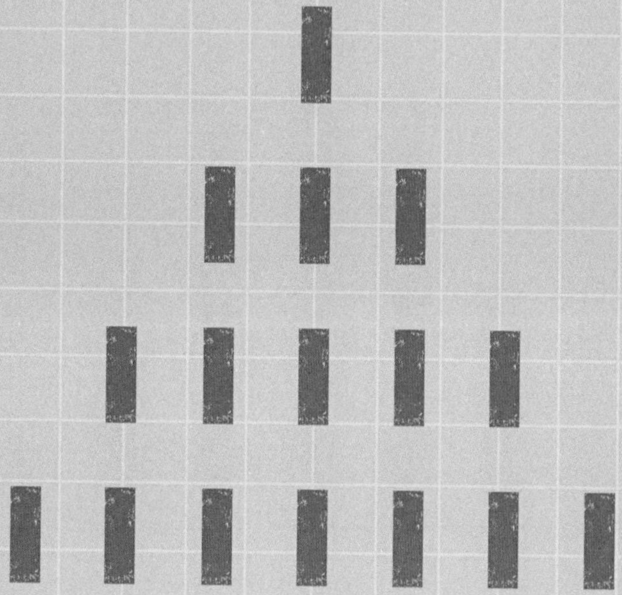

Game 2

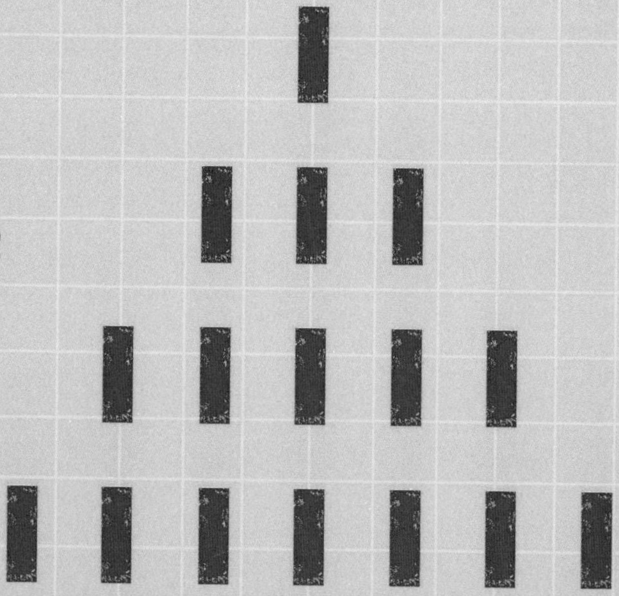

Strike out

Game 1

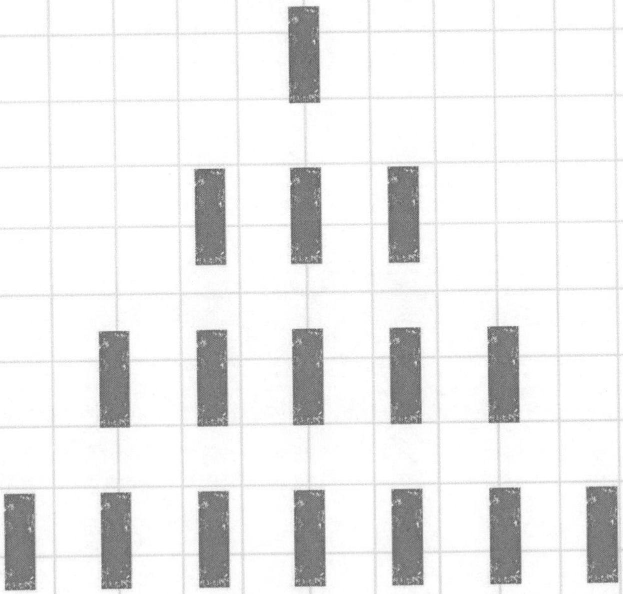

Game 2

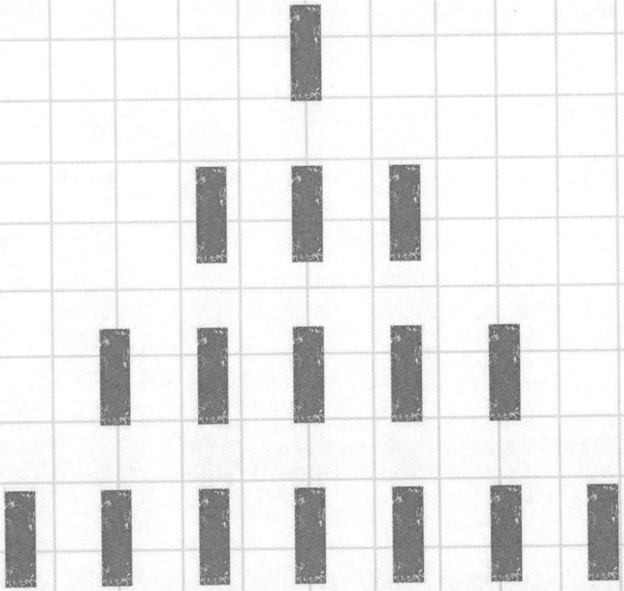

Strike out

72

Game 1

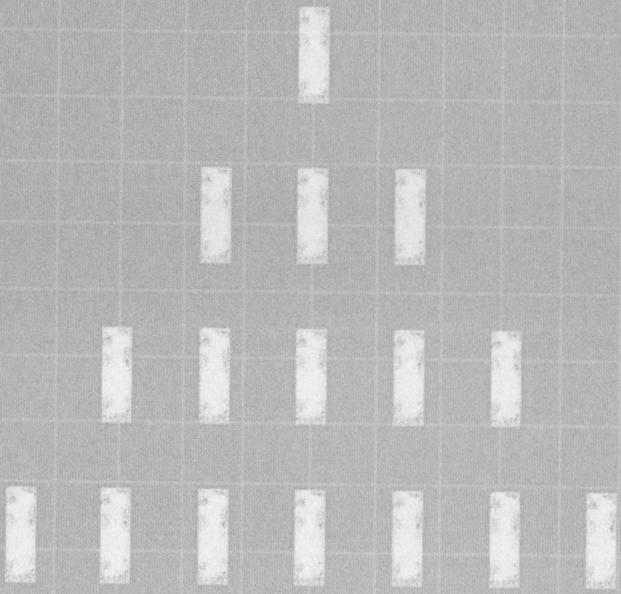

Game 2

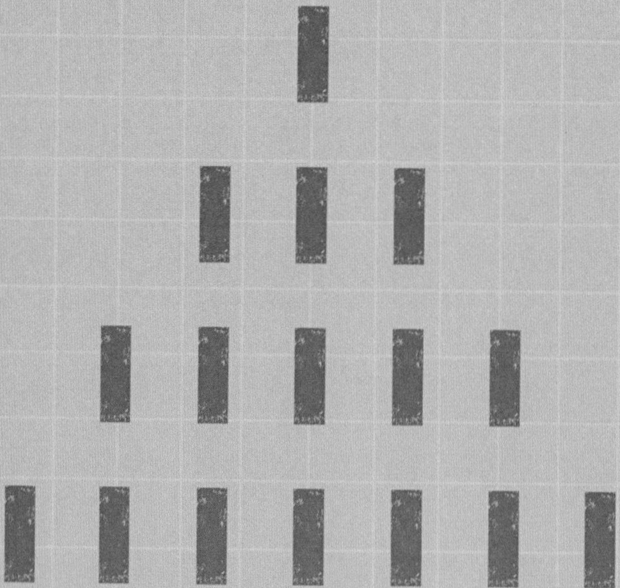

Strike out

Game 1

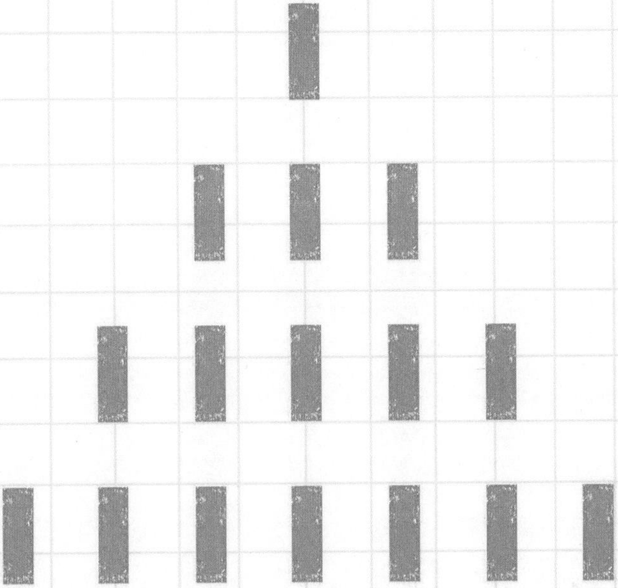

Game 2

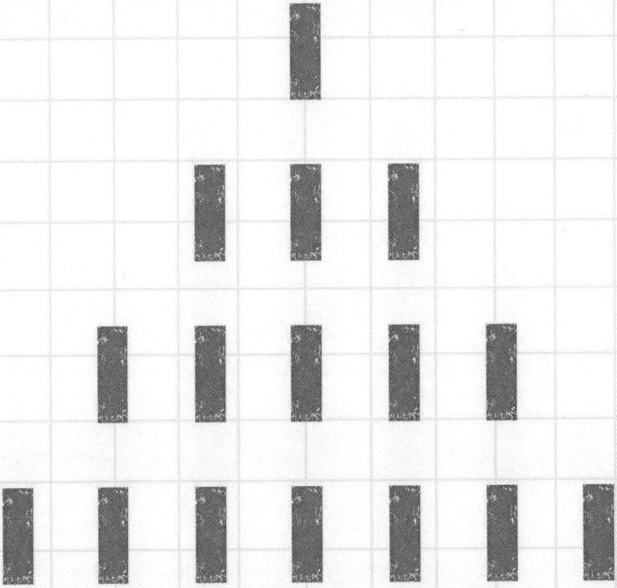

Strike out

Game 1

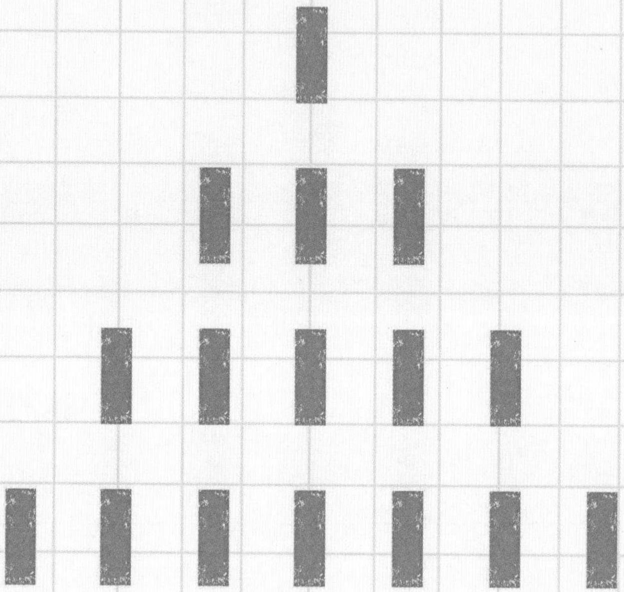

Game 2

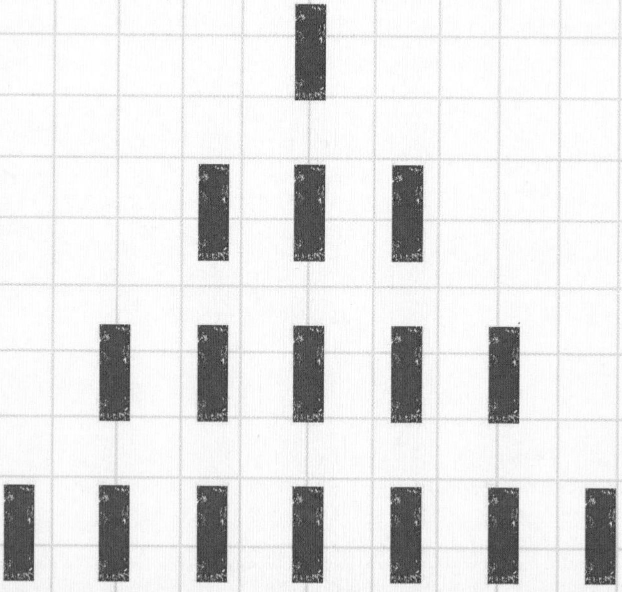

Strike out

75

Game 1

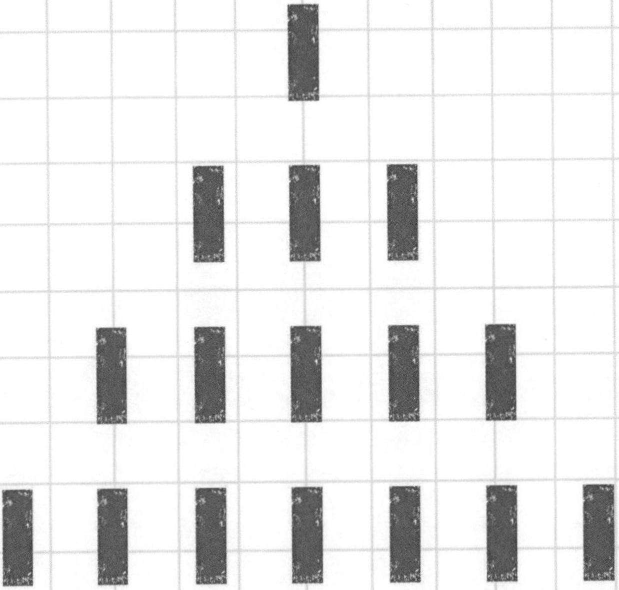

Game 2

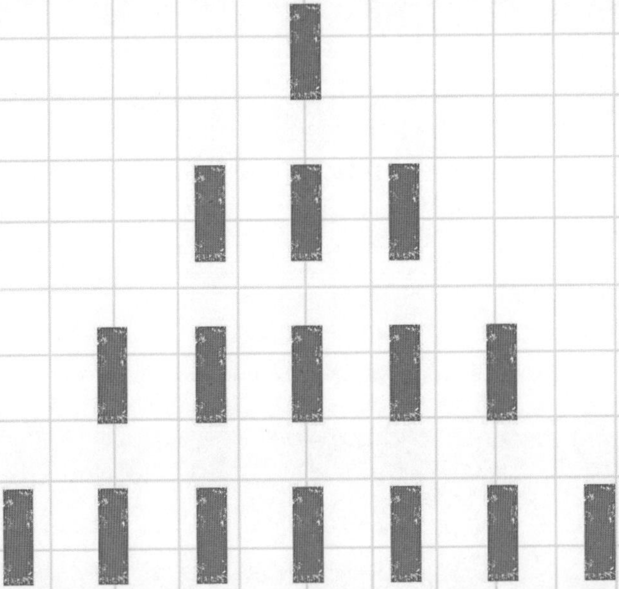

Strike out

Game 1

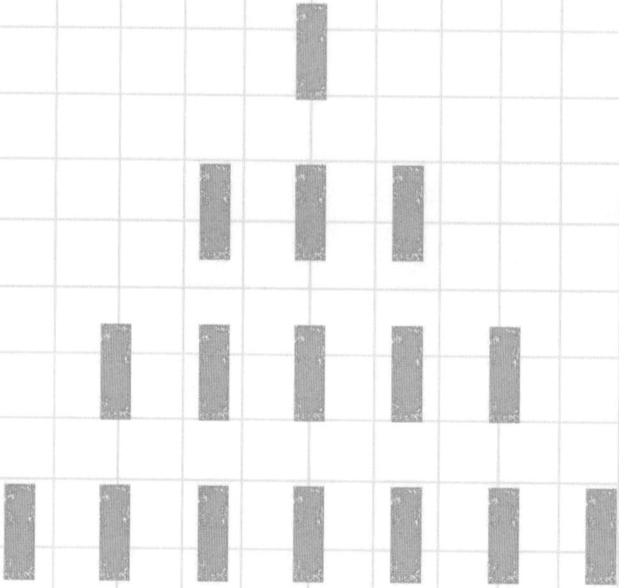

Game 2

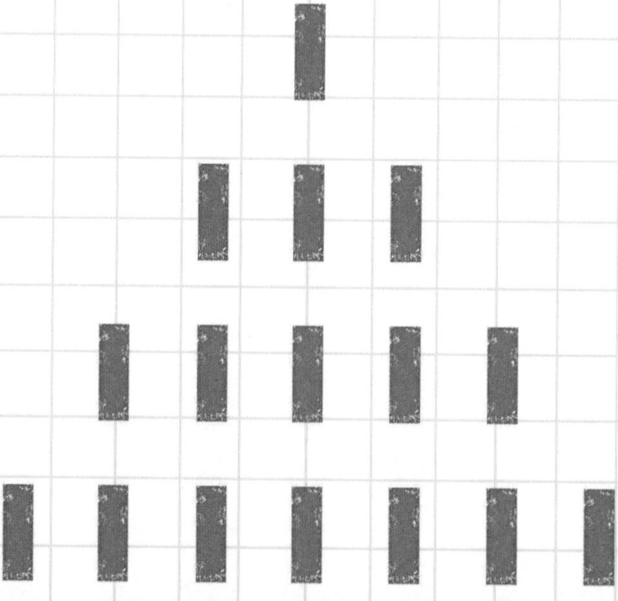

Code breaker instructions

Before you begin, cut or tear the page in two along the dotted line.

1. Player 1 takes the top part of the page and writes a secret four-digit code in the boxes. You must choose numbers between one and six, and you can't use the same number more than once.

2. Player 2 has their first try at guessing the code. Player 1 then puts a mark under the green circle for a number that's correct and in the right position, and a mark under the orange circle for a number that's correct but in the wrong position.

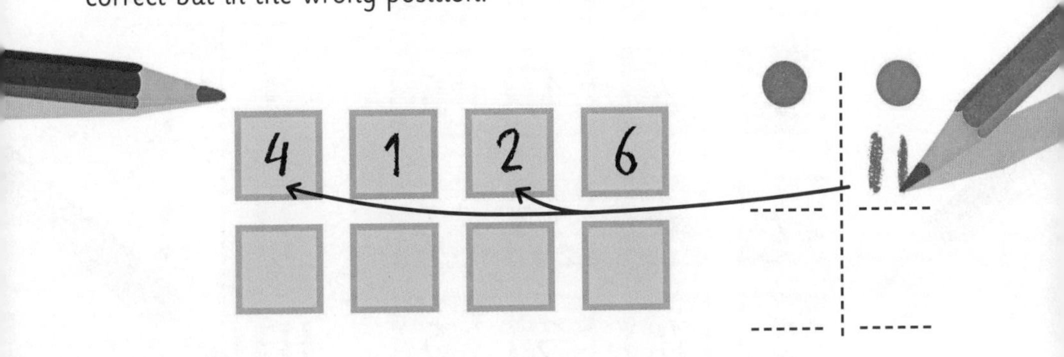

3 Player 2 has another guess, using the marks as clues. This time there are more correct numbers, but still none in the right place...

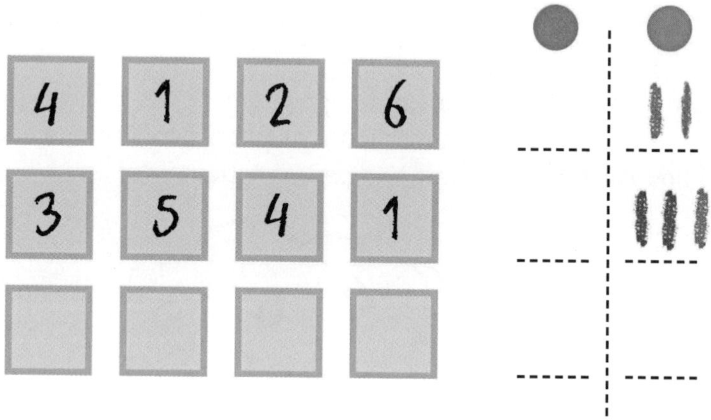

4 The goal is to crack the code in seven turns or less. Player 2 took five turns in this game.

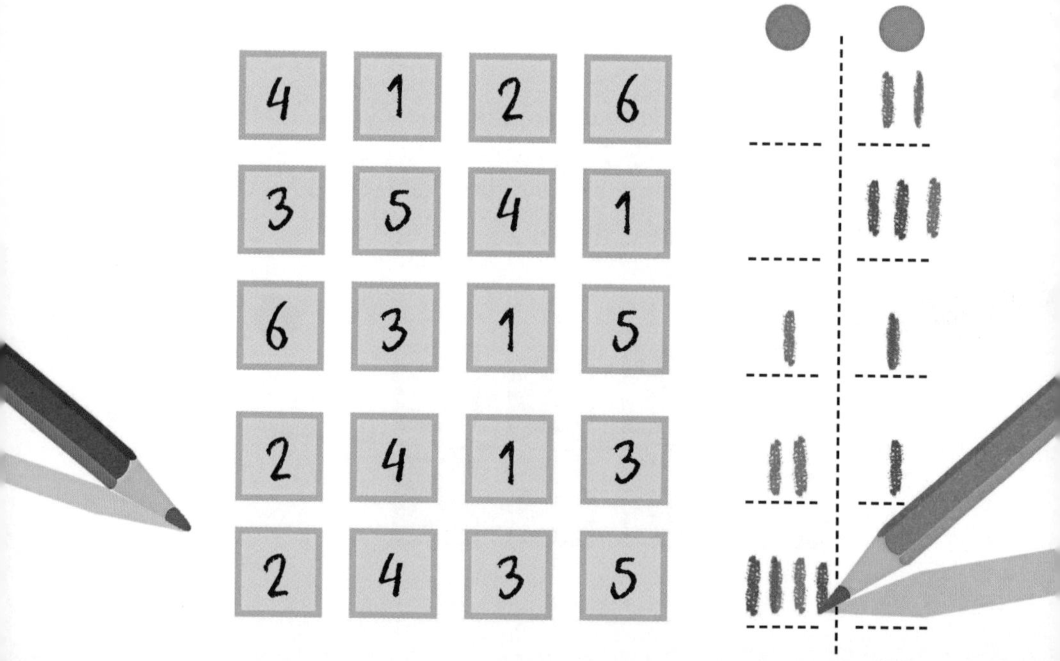

Code breaker

Cut or tear along the dotted line.

Secret file

Code breaker

Cut or tear along the dotted line.

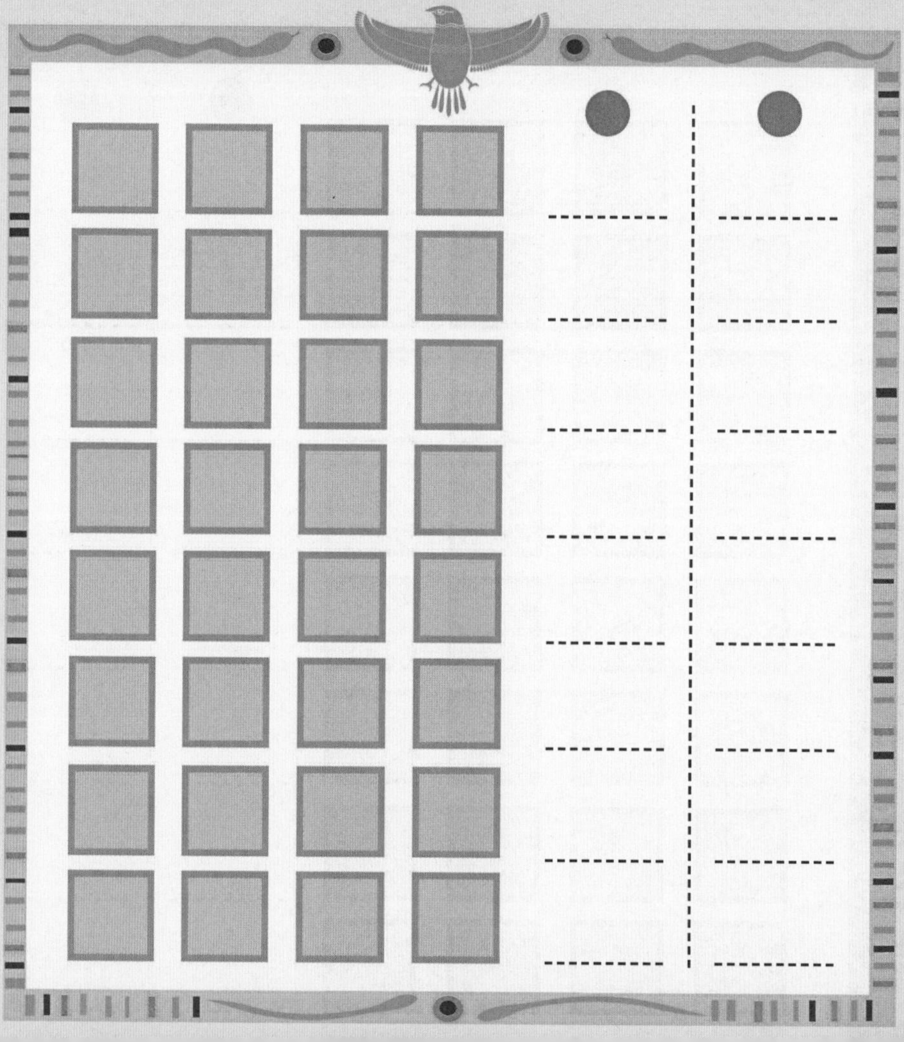

Code breaker

Cut or tear along the dotted line.

Code breaker

Cut or tear along the dotted line.

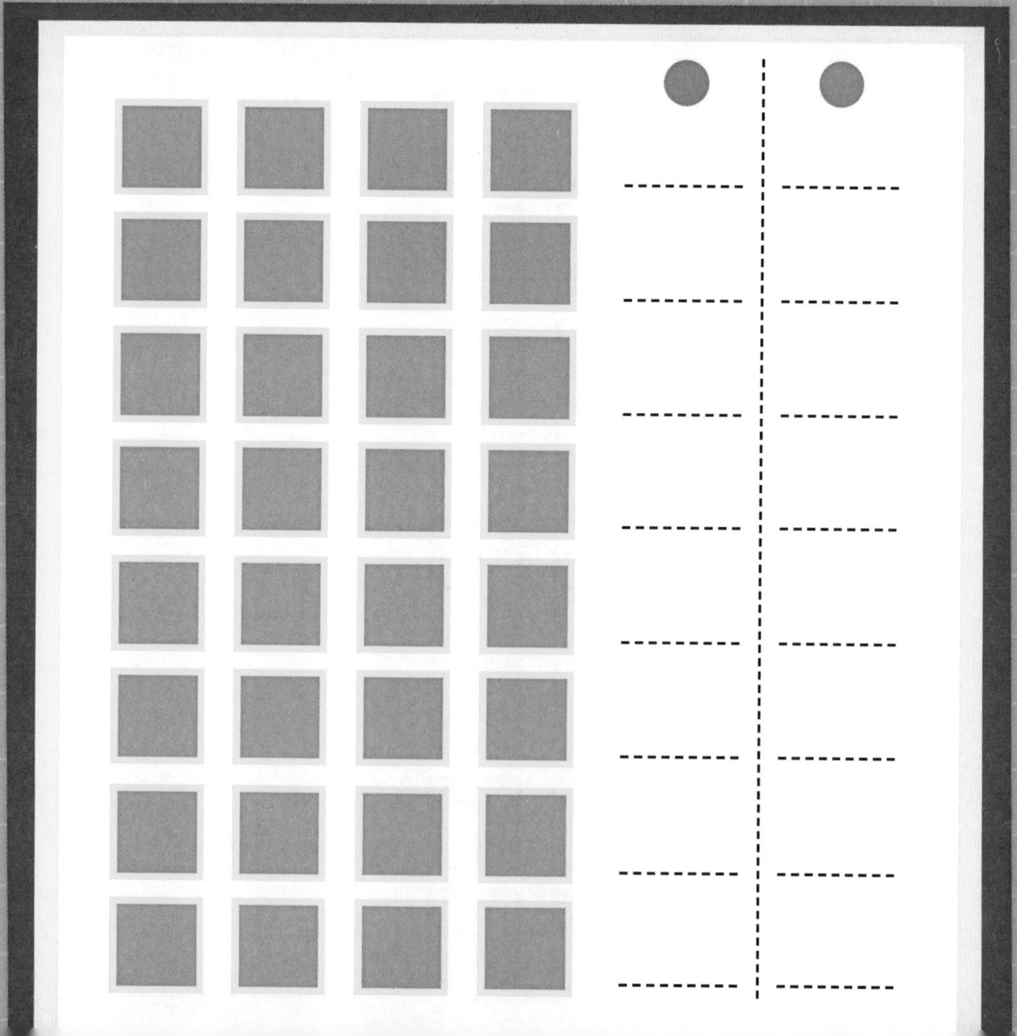

Code breaker

Cut or tear along the dotted line.

Code breaker

Cut or tear along the dotted line.

Code breaker

Cut or tear along the dotted line.

Code breaker

Cut or tear along the dotted line.

Sharp shooter instructions

86

1 Before the game begins, both players mark an 'X' anywhere along the borderline of their zone. This is your starting position.

2 The goal is to draw a line in one quick swipe from your starting position straight through your opponent's zone.

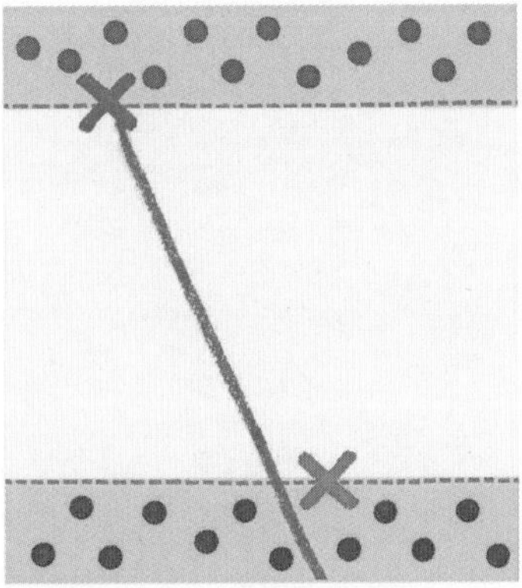

3 To score a point, your line must reach the back edge of your opponent's zone and not touch any dots on the way.

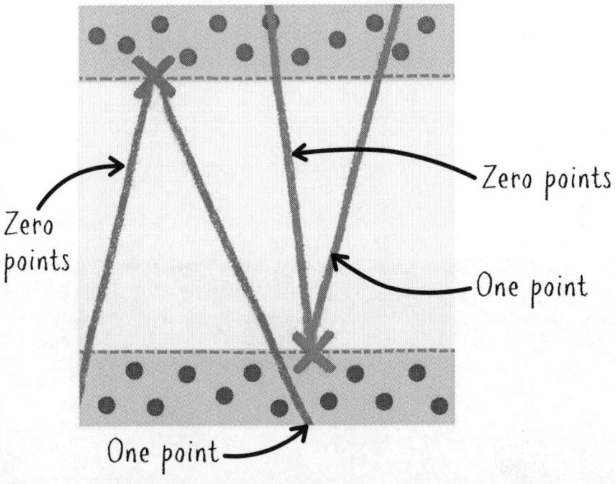

4 The first player to score five points is the winner. If both players reach five points in the same number of turns, the game is a tie.

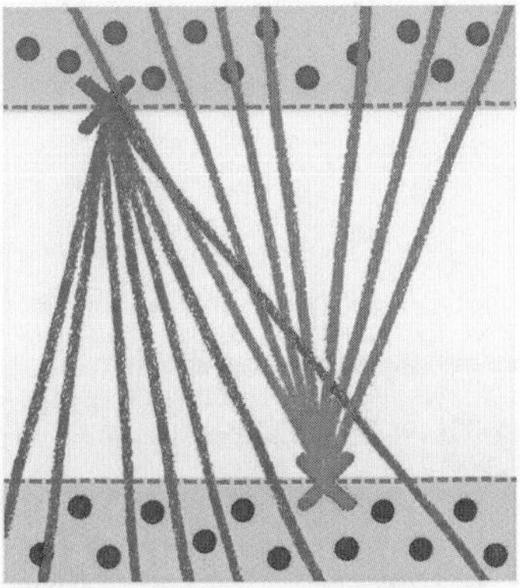

Player 1 (green) won this game.

Sharp shooter

Sharp shooter

Sharp shooter

Sharp shooter

Sharp shooter

Sharp shooter

Sharp shooter

Sharp shooter

Sharp shooter

Sharp shooter

Sharp shooter

Battleships instructions

Before you begin, cut or tear along the dotted line so that each player has their own pair of grids.

1. Draw three ships on your fleet grid without letting your opponent see them. The ships go horizontally or vertically in lines of 3, 4 and 5 squares.

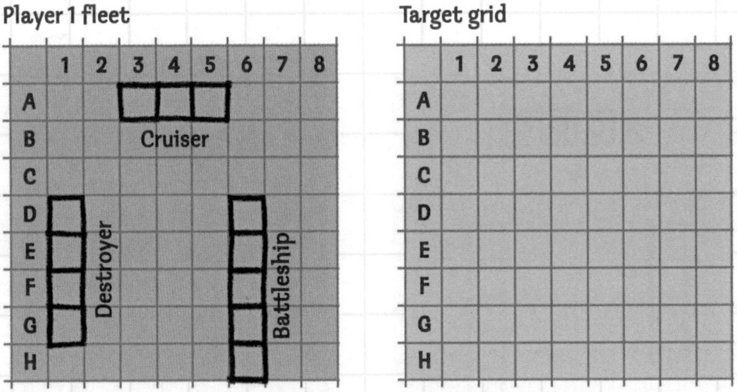

2. Take turns firing at each other. Mark your own shots on your target grid, and your opponent's shots on your fleet grid. Use X for a miss and O for a hit.

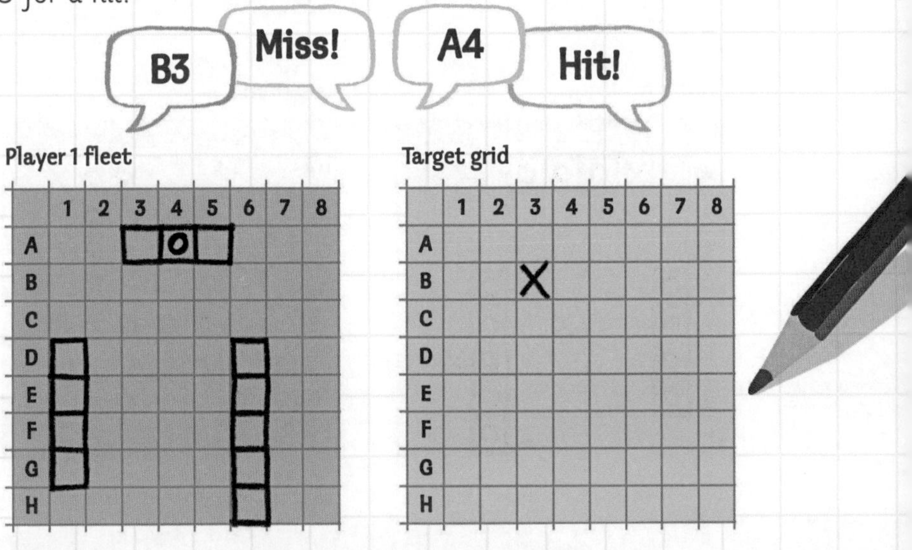

3 A ship is sunk when all its squares are hit. Tell your opponent which ship they've sunk.

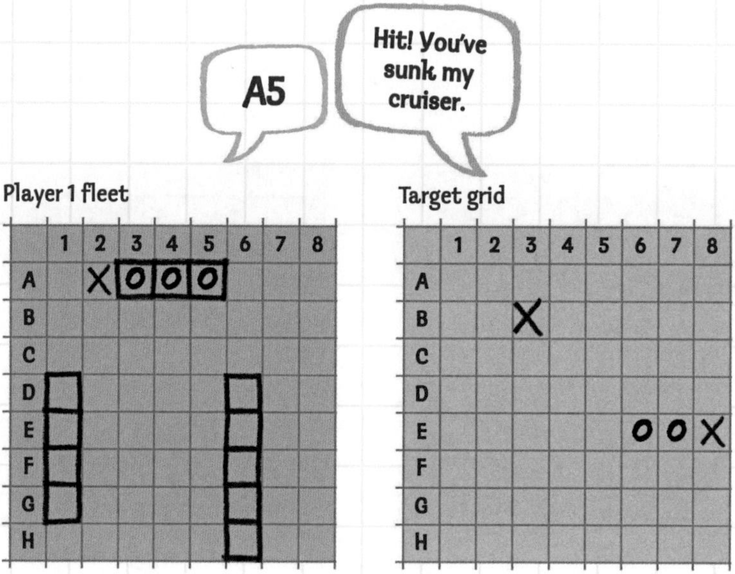

4 The first player to sink all of their opponent's ships is the winner. Player 2 won this game.

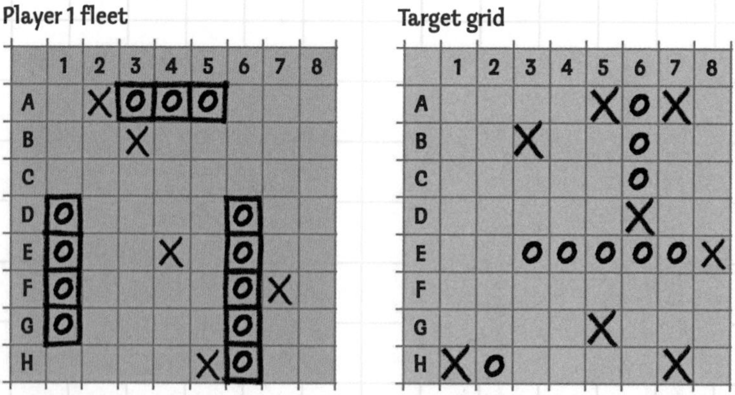

Battleships

Player 1 fleet

◎	1	2	3	4	5	6	7	8
A								
B								
C								
D								
E								
F								
G								
H								

Target grid

◎	1	2	3	4	5	6	7	8
A								
B								
C								
D								
E								
F								
G								
H								

Hit!

Cut or tear along the dotted line.

Player 2 fleet

◎	1	2	3	4	5	6	7	8
A								
B								
C								
D								
E								
F								
G								
H								

Target grid

◎	1	2	3	4	5	6	7	8
A								
B								
C								
D								
E								
F								
G								
H								

Battleships

Player 1 fleet

	1	2	3	4	5	6	7	8
A								
B								
C								
D								
E								
F								
G								
H								

Target grid

	1	2	3	4	5	6	7	8
A								
B								
C								
D								
E								
F								
G								
H								

Cut or tear along the dotted line.

Player 2 fleet

	1	2	3	4	5	6	7	8
A								
B								
C								
D								
E								
F								
G								
H								

Target grid

	1	2	3	4	5	6	7	8
A								
B								
C								
D								
E								
F								
G								
H								

Battleships

Player 1 fleet

	1	2	3	4	5	6	7	8
A								
B								
C								
D								
E								
F								
G								
H								

Target grid

	1	2	3	4	5	6	7	8
A								
B								
C								
D								
E								
F								
G								
H								

Cut or tear along the dotted line.

Player 2 fleet

	1	2	3	4	5	6	7	8
A								
B								
C								
D								
E								
F								
G								
H								

Target grid

	1	2	3	4	5	6	7	8
A								
B								
C								
D								
E								
F								
G								
H								

Battleships

Player 1 fleet

◎	1	2	3	4	5	6	7	8
A								
B								
C								
D								
E								
F								
G								
H								

Target grid

◎	1	2	3	4	5	6	7	8
A								
B								
C								
D								
E								
F								
G								
H								

Hit!

Cut or tear along the dotted line.

Miss!

Player 2 fleet

◎	1	2	3	4	5	6	7	8
A								
B								
C								
D								
E								
F								
G								
H								

Target grid

◎	1	2	3	4	5	6	7	8
A								
B								
C								
D								
E								
F								
G								
H								

Battleships

Player 1 fleet

	1	2	3	4	5	6	7	8
A								
B								
C								
D								
E								
F								
G								
H								

Target grid

	1	2	3	4	5	6	7	8
A								
B								
C								
D								
E								
F								
G								
H								

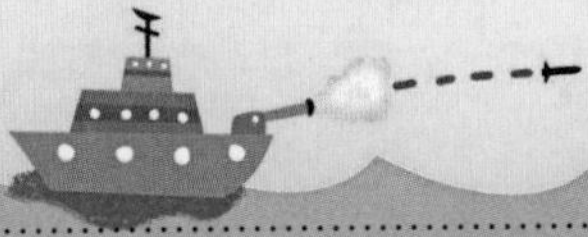

Cut or tear along the dotted line.

Player 2 fleet

	1	2	3	4	5	6	7	8
A								
B								
C								
D								
E								
F								
G								
H								

Target grid

	1	2	3	4	5	6	7	8
A								
B								
C								
D								
E								
F								
G								
H								

Battleships

Player 1 fleet

	1	2	3	4	5	6	7	8
A								
B								
C								
D								
E								
F								
G								
H								

Target grid

	1	2	3	4	5	6	7	8
A								
B								
C								
D								
E								
F								
G								
H								

Cut or tear along the dotted line.

Player 2 fleet

	1	2	3	4	5	6	7	8
A								
B								
C								
D								
E								
F								
G								
H								

Target grid

	1	2	3	4	5	6	7	8
A								
B								
C								
D								
E								
F								
G								
H								

Battleships

Miss!

Player 1 fleet

	1	2	3	4	5	6	7	8
A								
B								
C								
D								
E								
F								
G								
H								

Target grid

	1	2	3	4	5	6	7	8
A								
B								
C								
D								
E								
F								
G								
H								

Hit!

Cut or tear along the dotted line.

Player 2 fleet

	1	2	3	4	5	6	7	8
A								
B								
C								
D								
E								
F								
G								
H								

Target grid

	1	2	3	4	5	6	7	8
A								
B								
C								
D								
E								
F								
G								
H								

Battleships

Player 1 fleet

	1	2	3	4	5	6	7	8
A								
B								
C								
D								
E								
F								
G								
H								

Target grid

	1	2	3	4	5	6	7	8
A								
B								
C								
D								
E								
F								
G								
H								

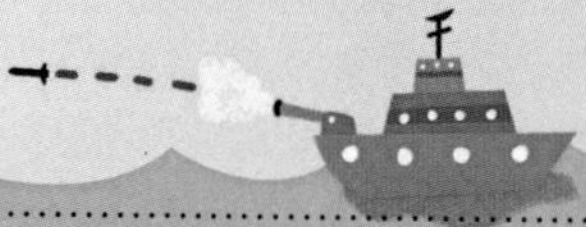

Cut or tear along the dotted line.

Player 2 fleet

	1	2	3	4	5	6	7	8
A								
B								
C								
D								
E								
F								
G								
H								

Target grid

	1	2	3	4	5	6	7	8
A								
B								
C								
D								
E								
F								
G								
H								

Battleships

Player 1 fleet

	1	2	3	4	5	6	7	8
A								
B								
C								
D								
E								
F								
G								
H								

Target grid

	1	2	3	4	5	6	7	8
A								
B								
C								
D								
E								
F								
G								
H								

Cut or tear along the dotted line.

Player 2 fleet

	1	2	3	4	5	6	7	8
A								
B								
C								
D								
E								
F								
G								
H								

Target grid

	1	2	3	4	5	6	7	8
A								
B								
C								
D								
E								
F								
G								
H								

Battleships

Player 1 fleet

	1	2	3	4	5	6	7	8
A								
B								
C								
D								
E								
F								
G								
H								

Target grid

	1	2	3	4	5	6	7	8
A								
B								
C								
D								
E								
F								
G								
H								

Cut or tear along the dotted line.

Player 2 fleet

	1	2	3	4	5	6	7	8
A								
B								
C								
D								
E								
F								
G								
H								

Target grid

	1	2	3	4	5	6	7	8
A								
B								
C								
D								
E								
F								
G								
H								

Caterpillar instructions

1. Player 1 (red) starts by drawing a line between two dots. The line can be vertical or horizontal.

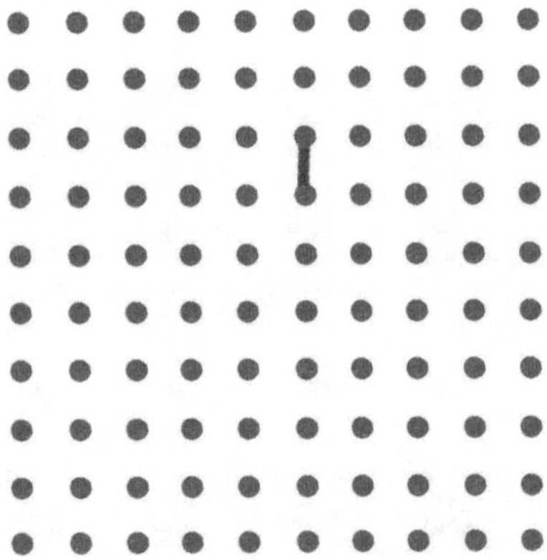

2. Player 2 (green) then joins one end of the line to another dot.

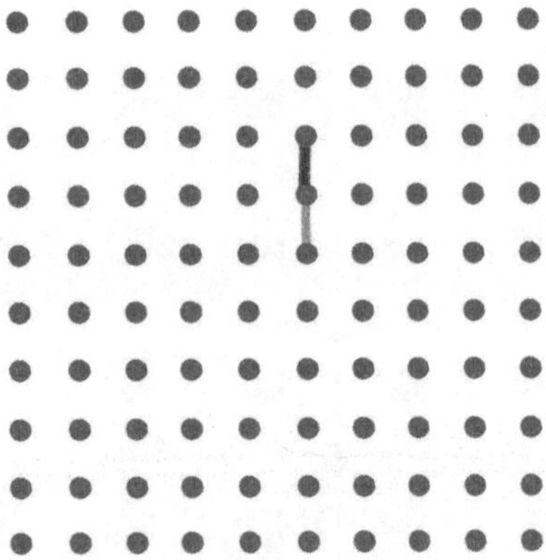

3. Take turns until one of you can't join either end of the line to a dot that hasn't been used. This player loses the game.

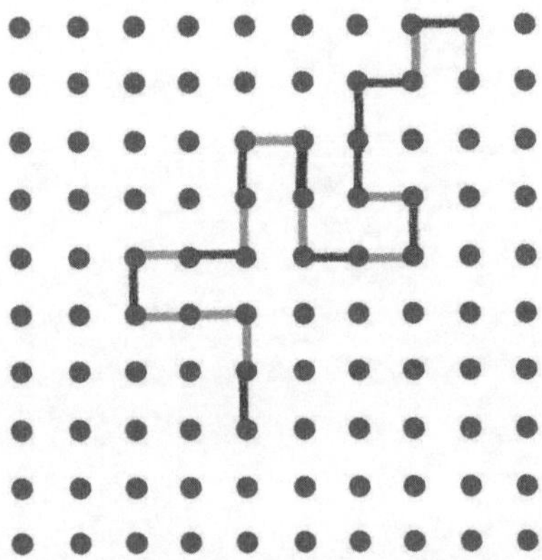

4. Player 1 wins the game below, because Player 2 can't connect to a dot that hasn't been used at either end of the line.

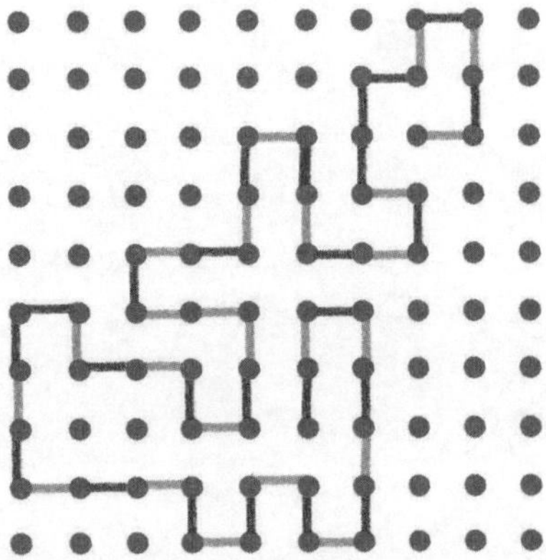

Caterpillar

110

Caterpillar

111

Caterpillar

112

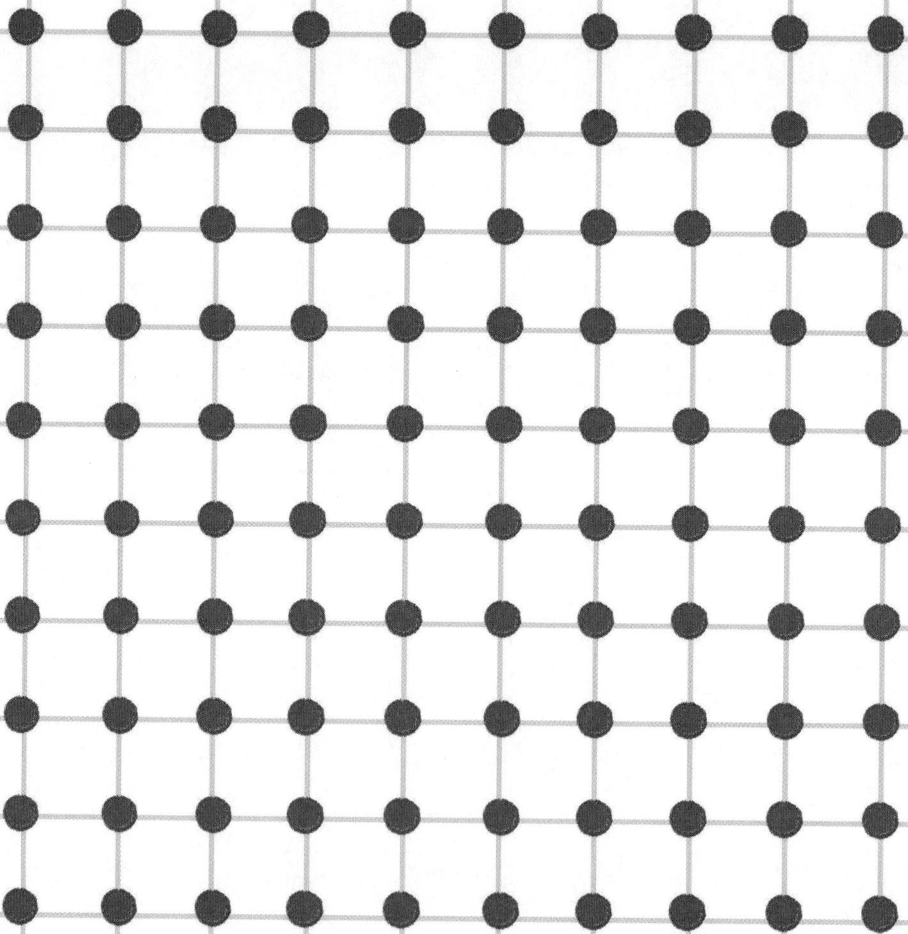

Caterpillar

Caterpillar

114

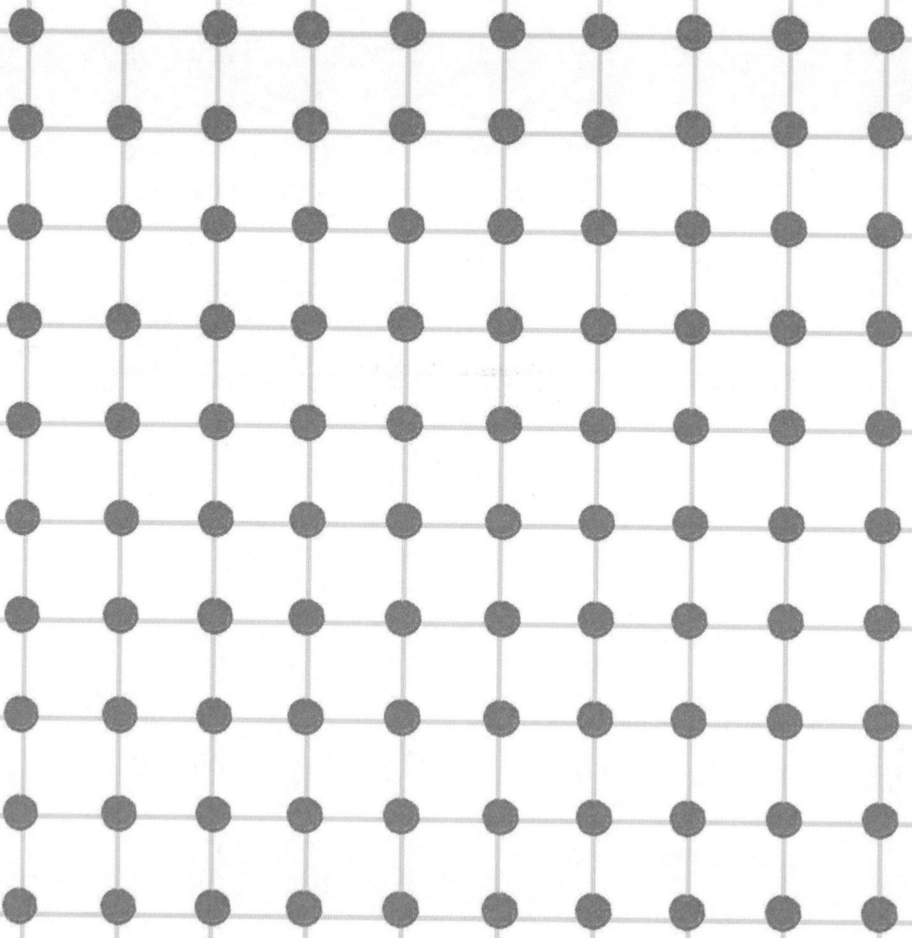

Caterpillar

Caterpillar

Caterpillar

117

Caterpillar

118

Shooting stars instructions

1 Before the game begins, each player draws a small circle anywhere along the start line. This is your starting position.

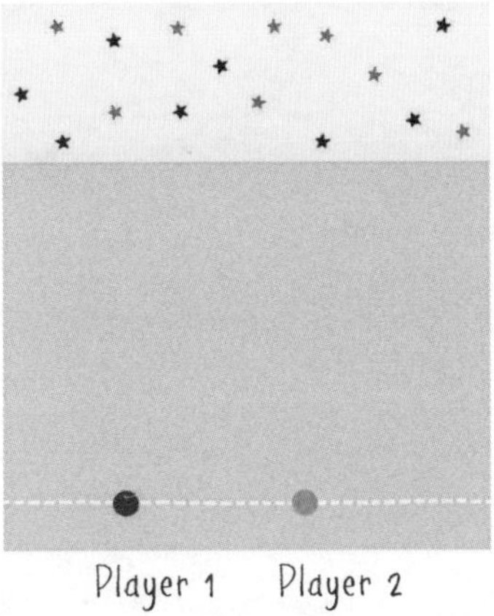

2 The goal is to hit a star by drawing a straight line in one quick swipe. In this game, Player 1 aims at the purple stars, Player 2 at the blue.

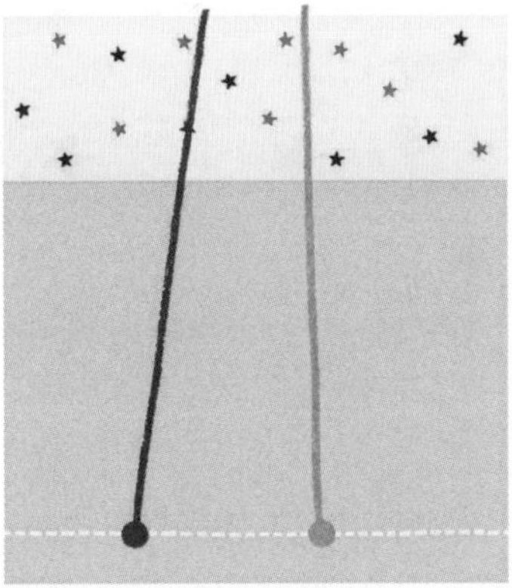

3 Score a point for each star you hit. But if you also hit your opponent's star with the same line, score zero points. If you hit two of your own stars, score two points.

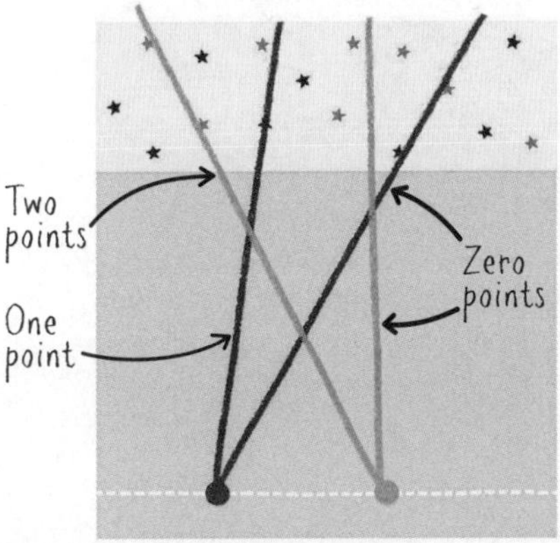

4 The first player to score three points is the winner. If both players reach three points in the same number of turns, the game is a tie. Player 2 won this game.

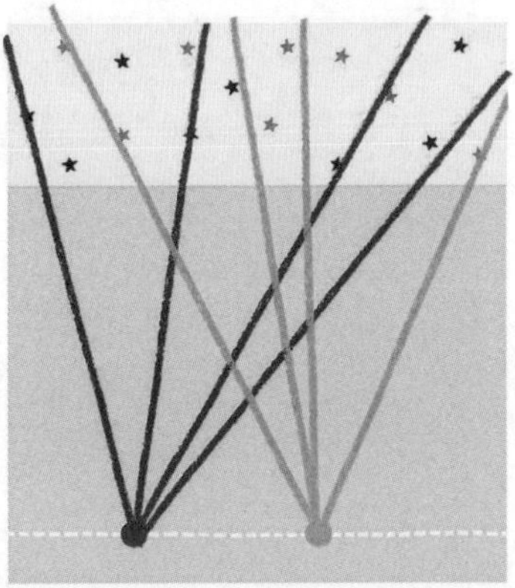

Shooting stars

Shooting stars

Shooting stars

122

Shooting stars

123

Shooting stars

124

Shooting stars

125

Shooting stars

126

Super Os and Xs instructions

1. Player 1 marks an X in any of the spaces on the grid.

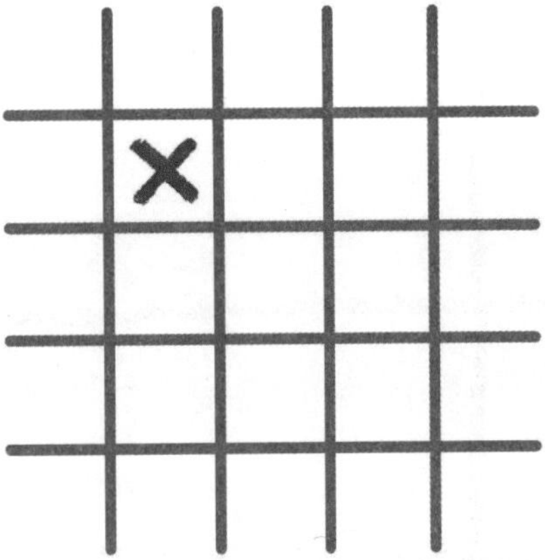

2. Player 2 then marks an O in any of the other spaces.

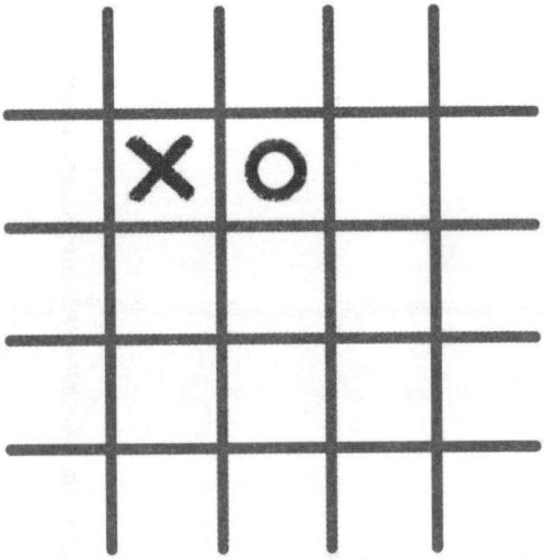

3. The goal is to make horizontal, vertical or diagonal lines of three in a row. You can't reuse one of your symbols to make another line.

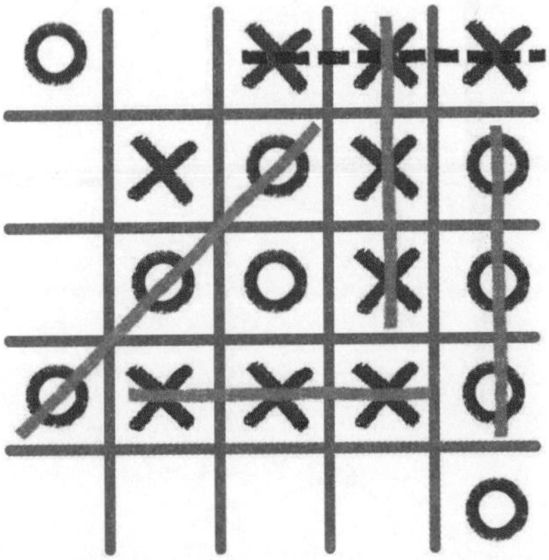

4. The winner is the player who makes the most lines of three in a row. Player 1 won this game.

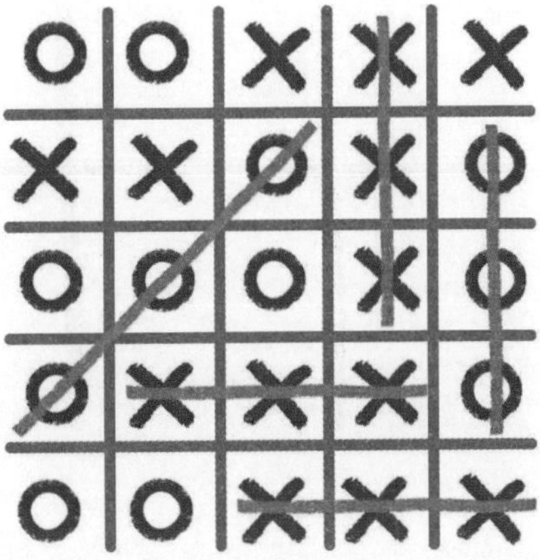

Super Os and Xs

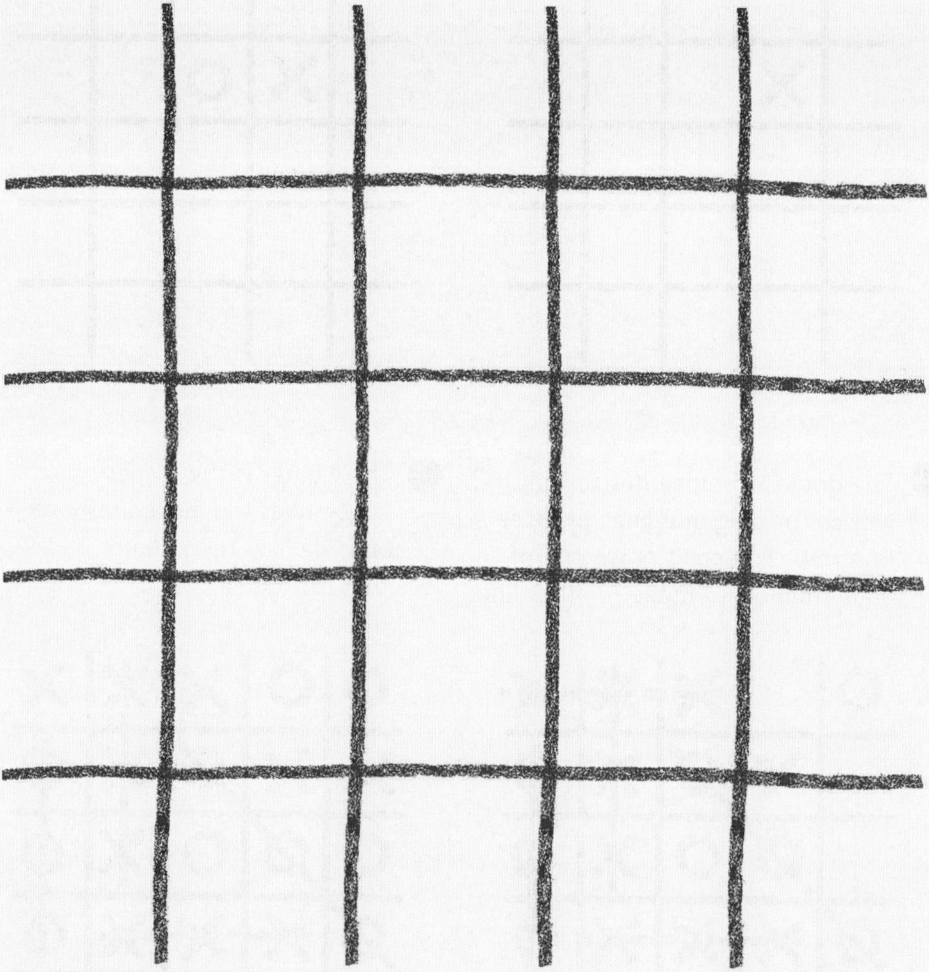

Super Os and Xs

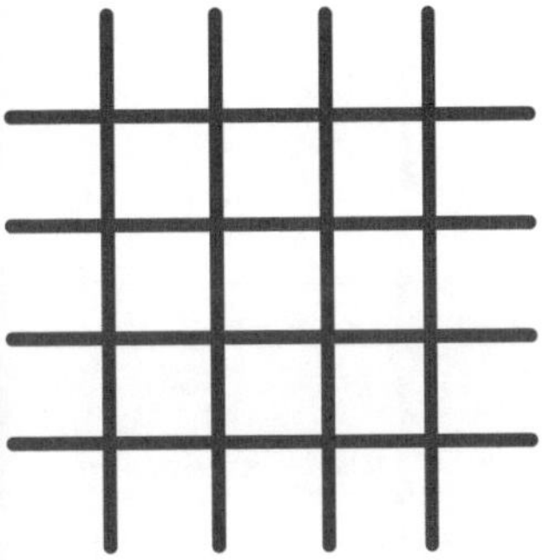
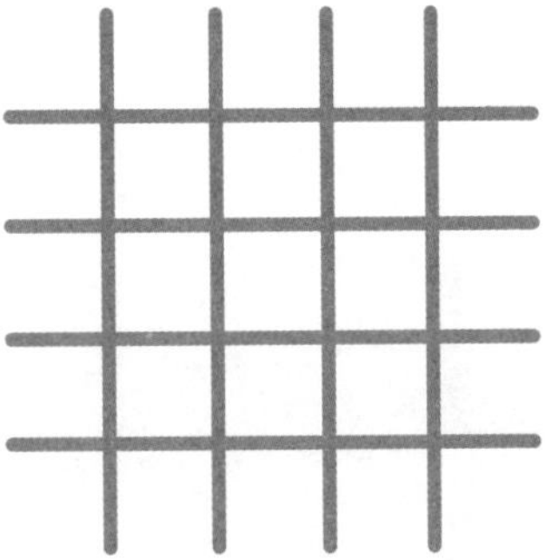
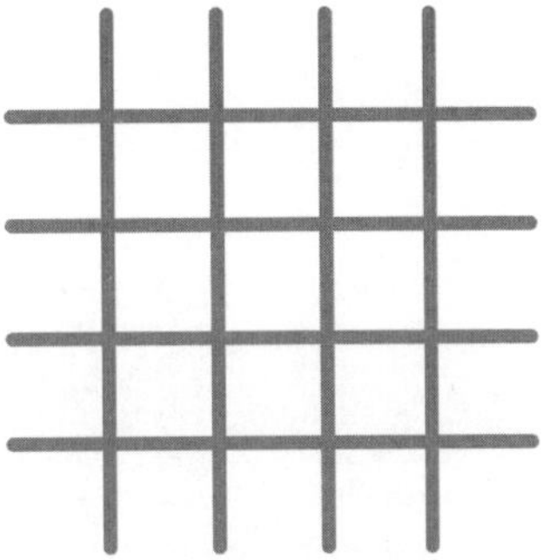
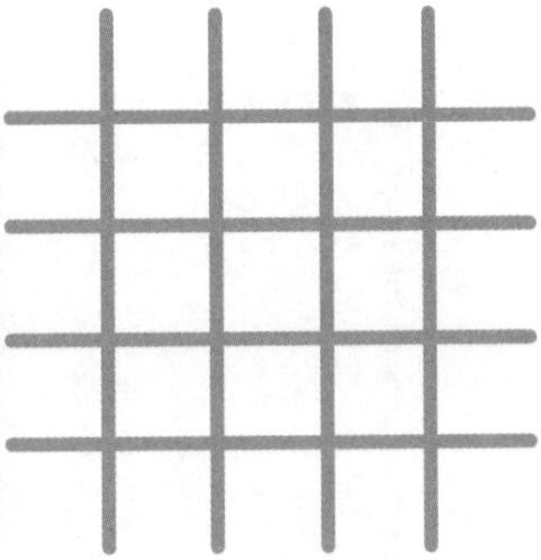
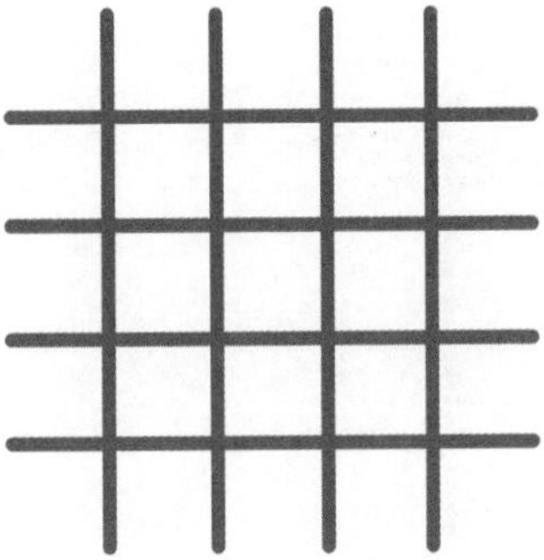

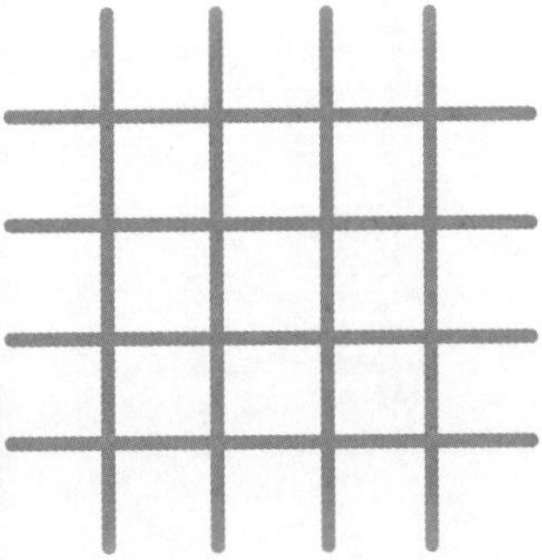
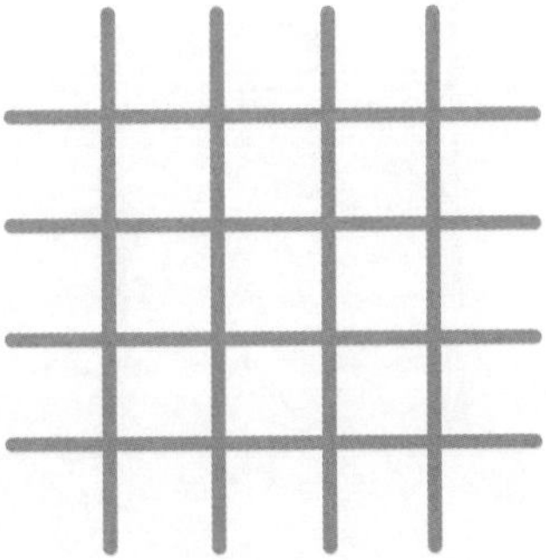
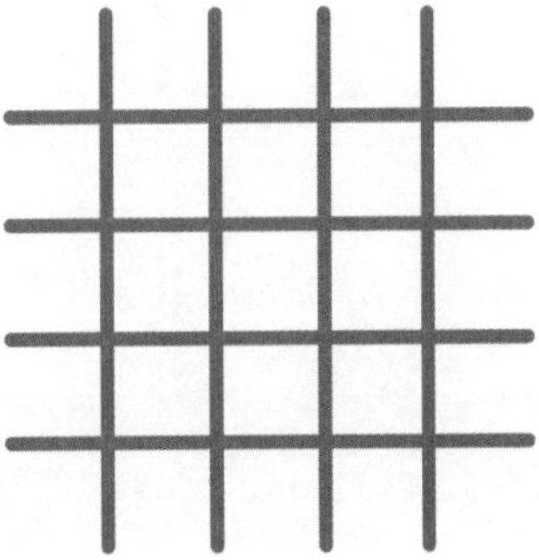

Super Os and Xs

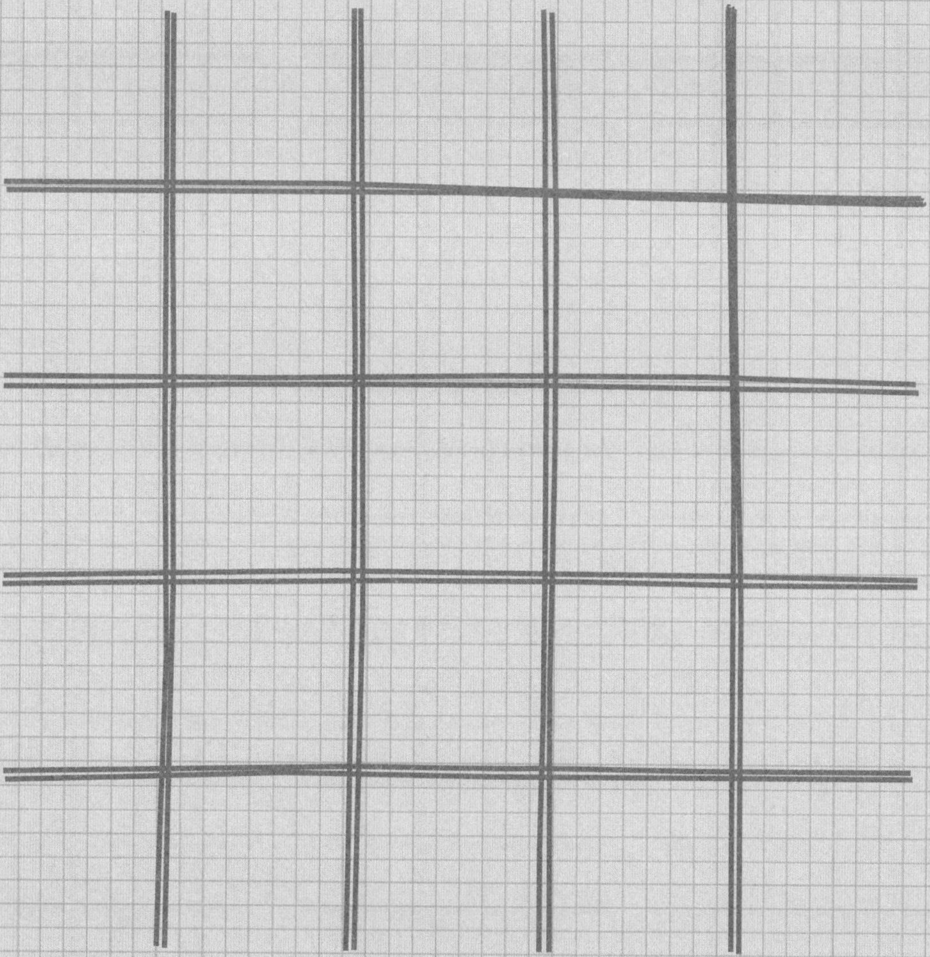

Super Os and Xs

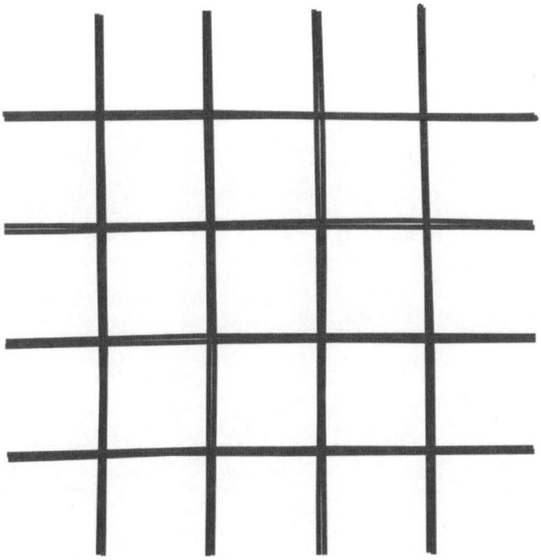

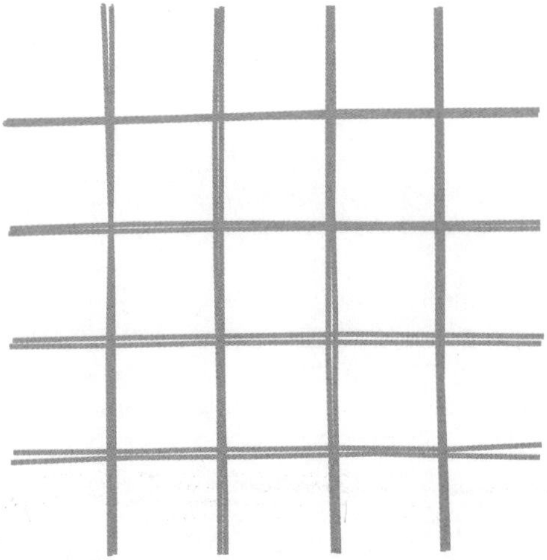

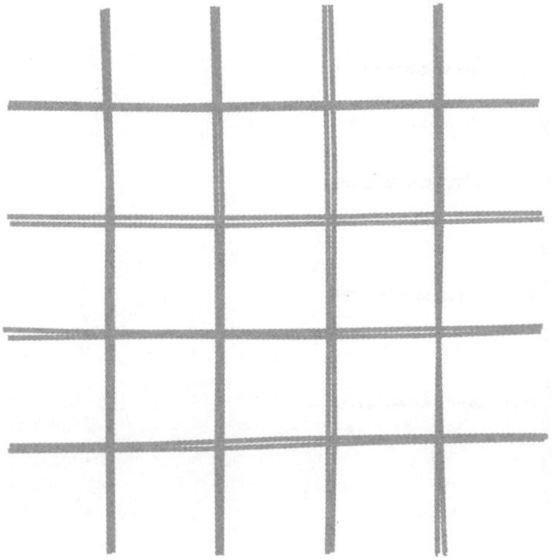

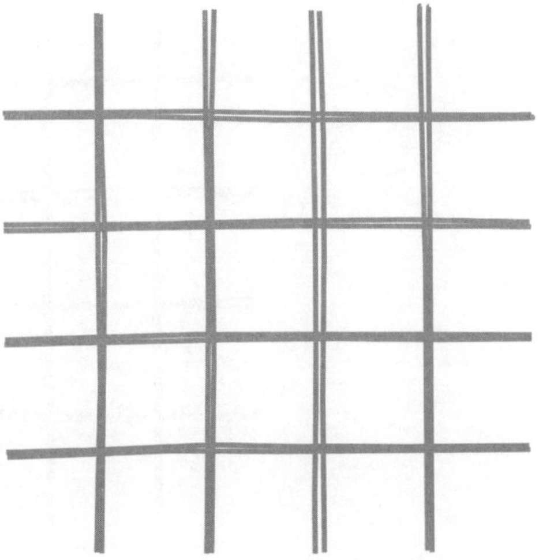

Super Os and Xs

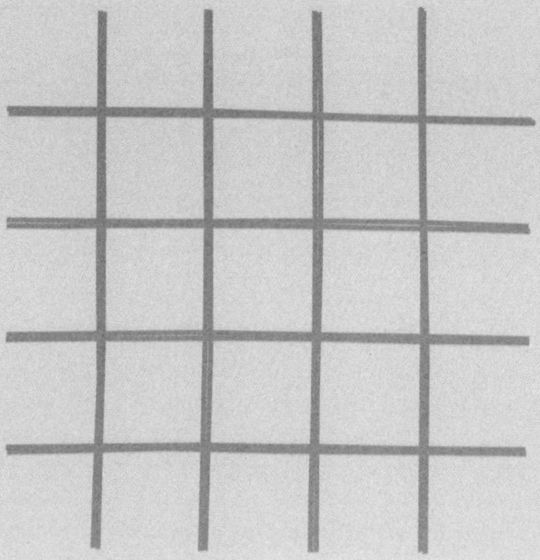

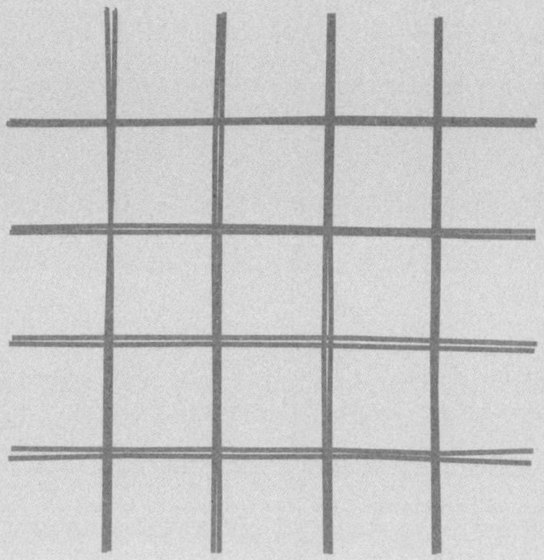

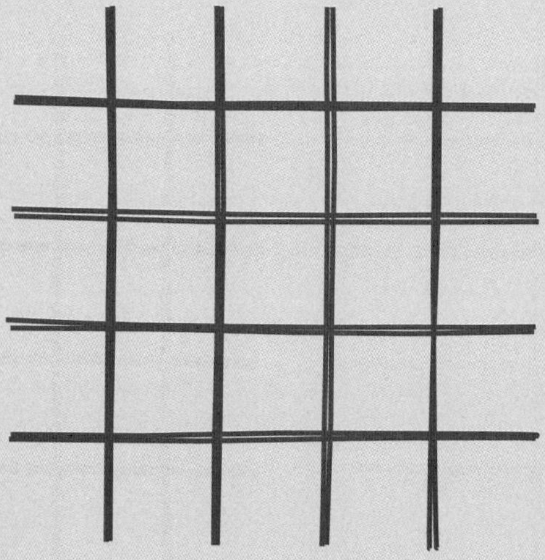

Super Os and Xs

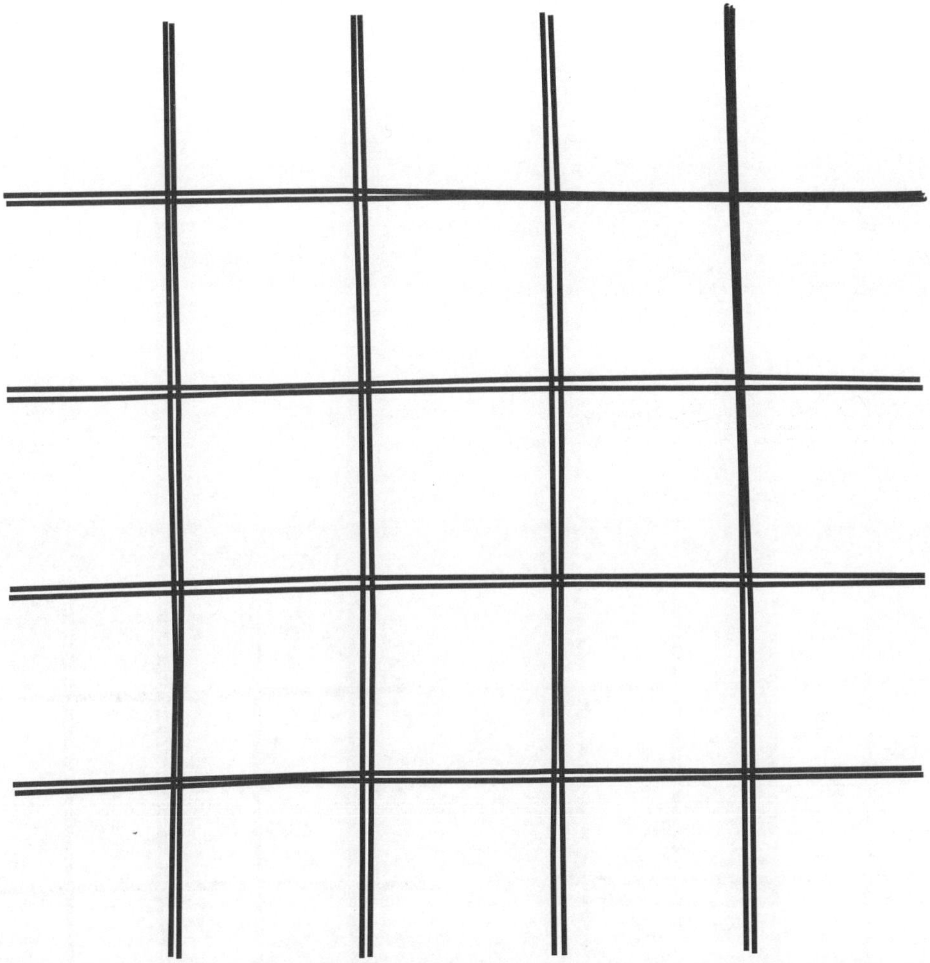

Super Os and Xs

134

Super Os and Xs

Super Os and Xs

Crossed words instructions

1. Player 1 thinks of a word, then writes it down and crosses out all those letters from the top alphabet.

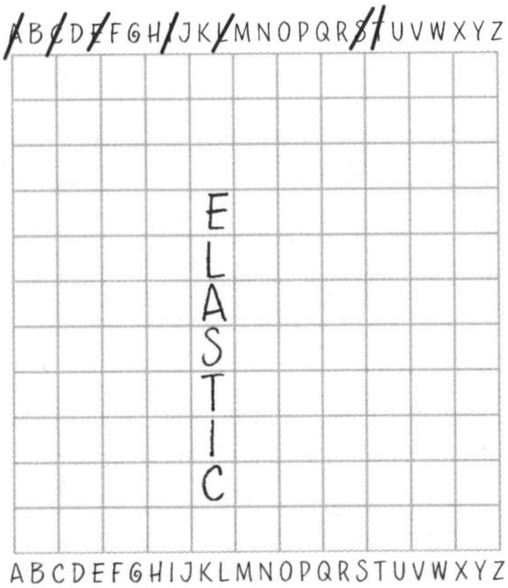

2. Player 2 joins a word to the first word and crosses out all those letters from the bottom alphabet (except for the one used in the first word).

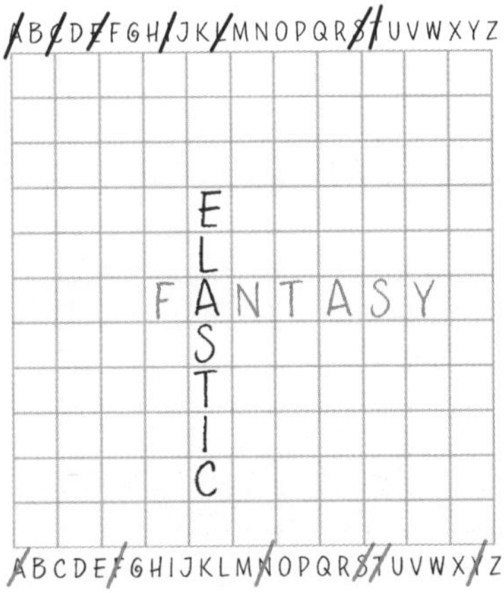

3. You can't play a letter more than once, and words can't go side by side unless each pair of letters makes a new word.

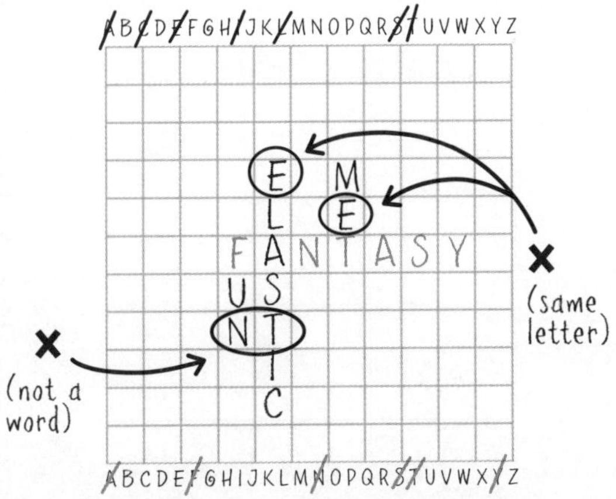

4. The game ends when neither player can use any more letters. The player who's used the most letters is the winner. Player 2 won this game.

Crossed words

a b c d e f g h i j k l m n o p q r s t u v w x y z

a b c d e f g h i j k l m n o p q r s t u v w x y z

Crossed words

a b c d e f g h i j k l m n o p q r s t u v w x y z

a b c d e f g h i j k l m n o p q r s t u v w x y z

Crossed words

a b c d e f g h i j k l m n o p q r s t u v w x y z

a b c d e f g h i j k l m n o p q r s t u v w x y z

Crossed words

141

A B C D E F G H I J K L M N O P Q R S T U V W X Y Z

A B C D E F G H I J K L M N O P Q R S T U V W X Y Z

Crossed words

a b c d e f g h i j k l m n o p q r s t u v w x y z

a b c d e f g h i j k l m n o p q r s t u v w x y z

Crossed words

A B C D E F G H I J K L M N O P Q R S T U V W X Y Z

A B C D E F G H I J K L M N O P Q R S T U V W X Y Z

Crossed words

A B C D E F G H I J K L M N O P Q R S T U V W X Y Z

A B C D E F G H I J K L M N O P Q R S T U V W X Y Z

Crossed words

a b c d e f g h i j k l m n o p q r s t u v w x y z

a b c d e f g h i j k l m n o p q r s t u v w x y z

Crossed words

146

a b c d e f g h i j k l m n o p q r s t u v w x y z

a b c d e f g h i j k l m n o p q r s t u v w x y z

Crossed words

a b c d e f g h i j k l m n o p q r s t u v w x y z

a b c d e f g h i j k l m n o p q r s t u v w x y z

Crossed words

a b c d e f g h i j k l m n o p q r s t u v w x y z

a b c d e f g h i j k l m n o p q r s t u v w x y z

Boxes instructions

1. Player 1 (green) joins any two dots with a horizontal or vertical straight line.

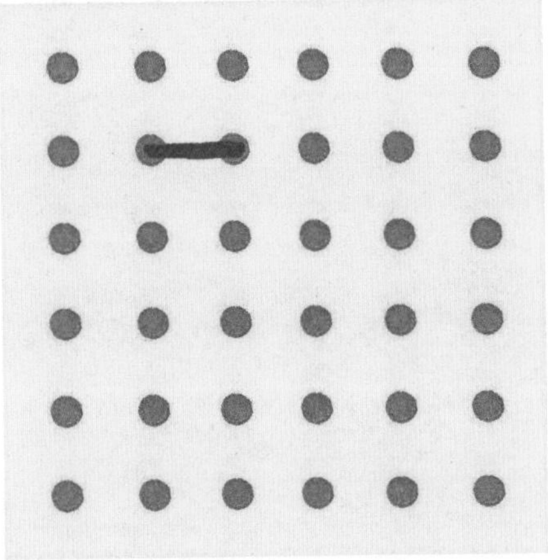

2. Player 2 (orange) then makes another horizontal or vertical straight line.

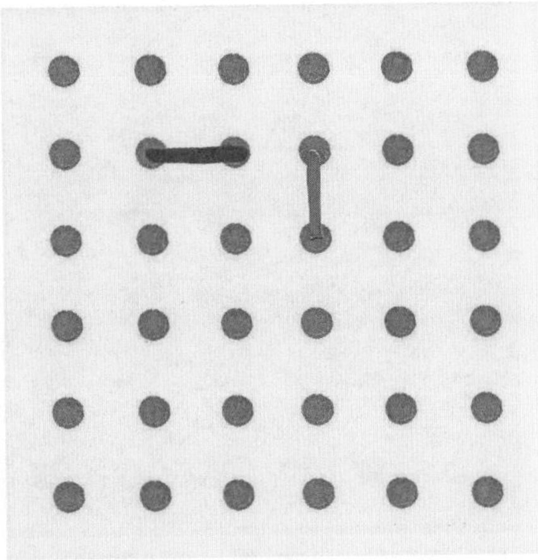

3. The goal is to be the player that completes a box. When you complete a box, write your initial inside and take an extra turn.

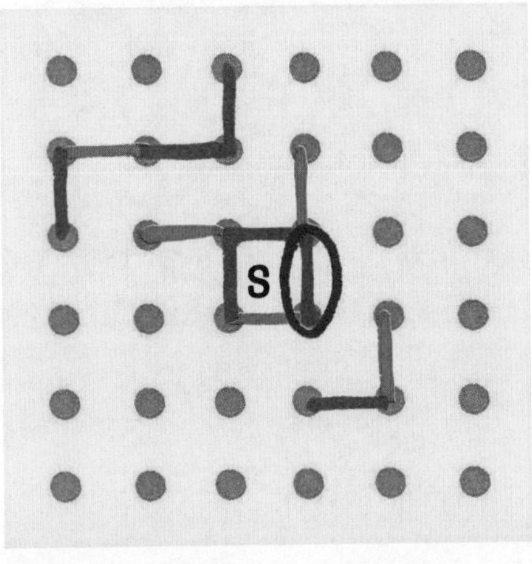

4. When no more lines can be added, the winner is the player who's made the most boxes. Player 1 won this game.

Boxes

150

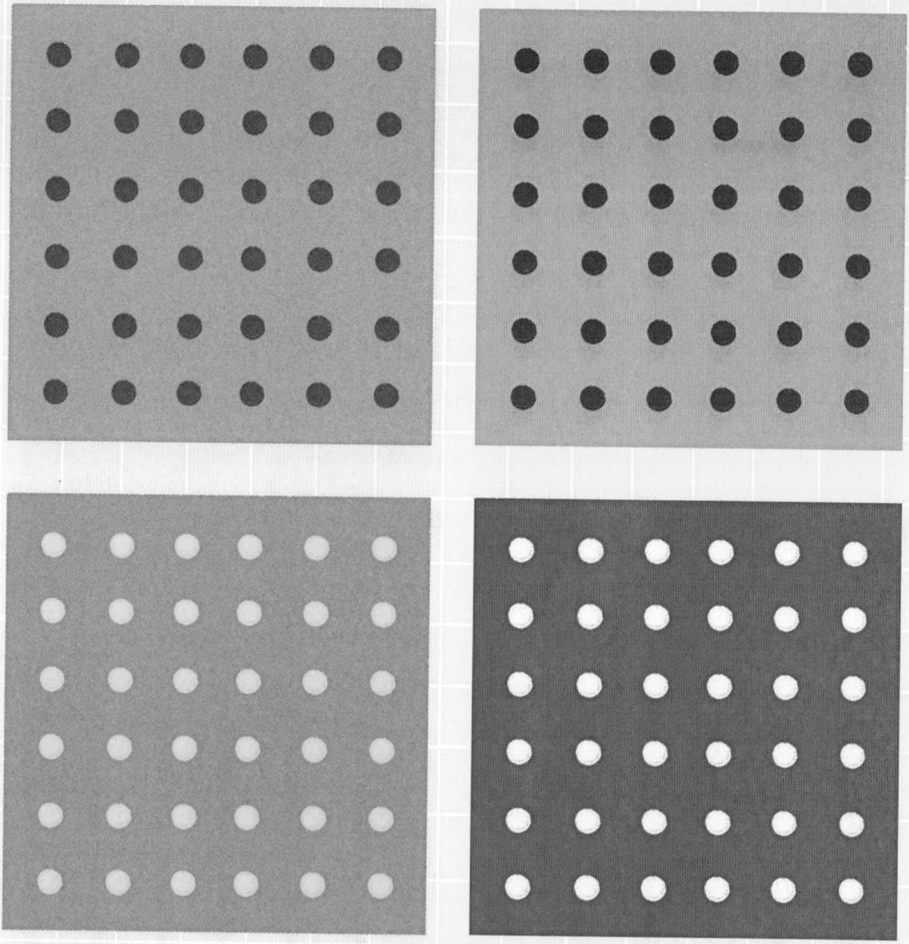

Boxes

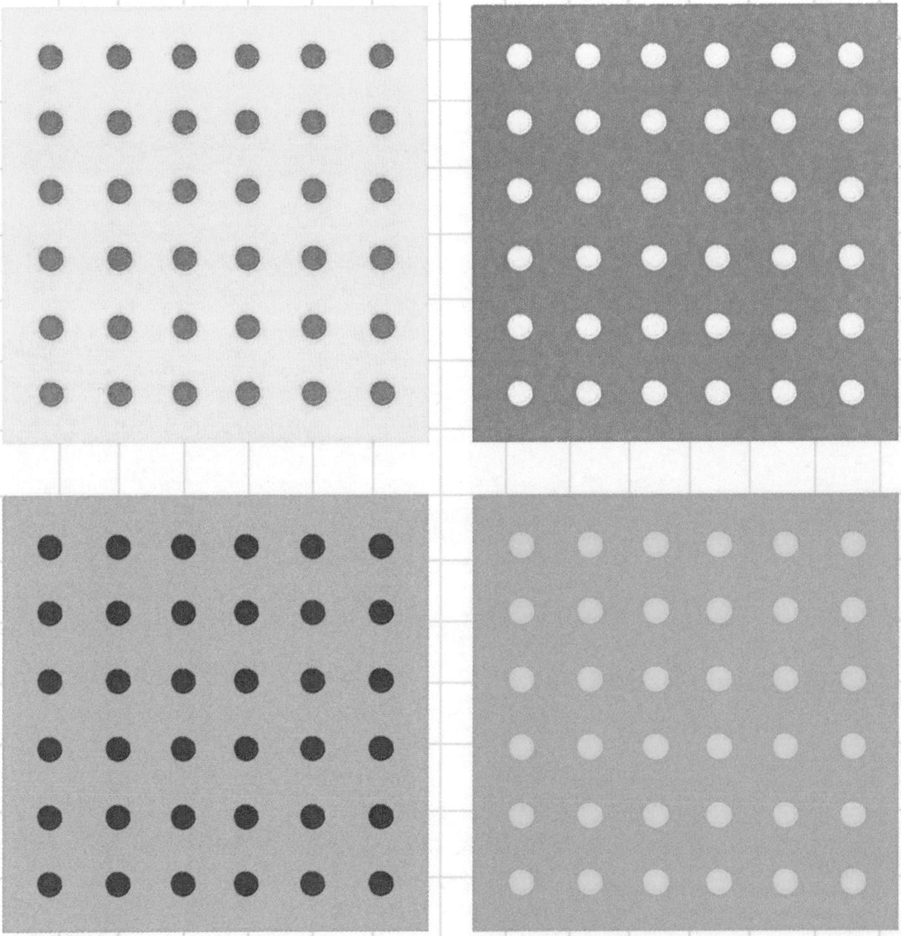

Boxes

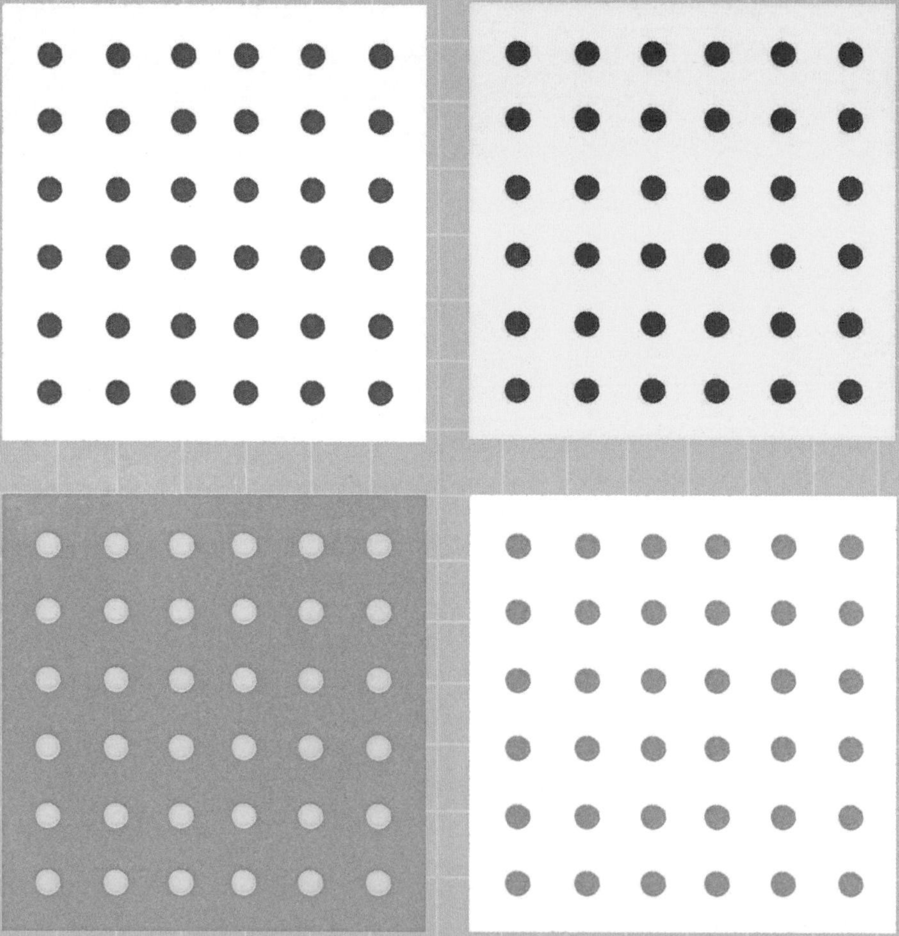

Boxes

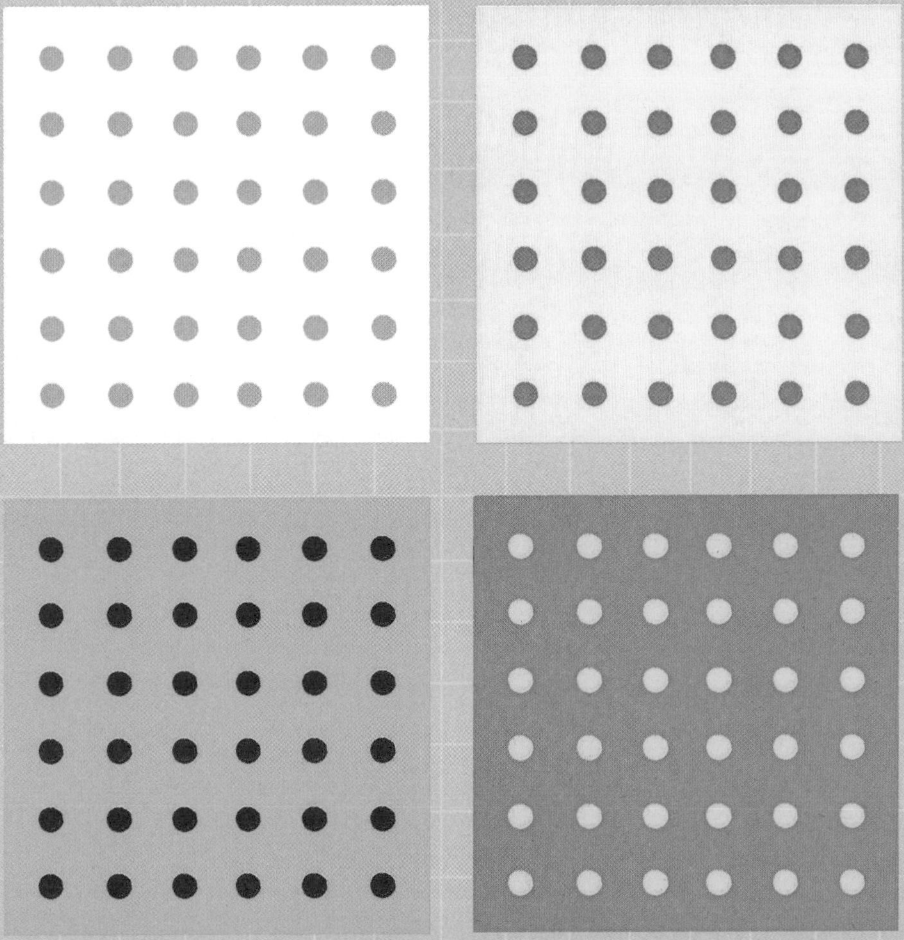

Boxes

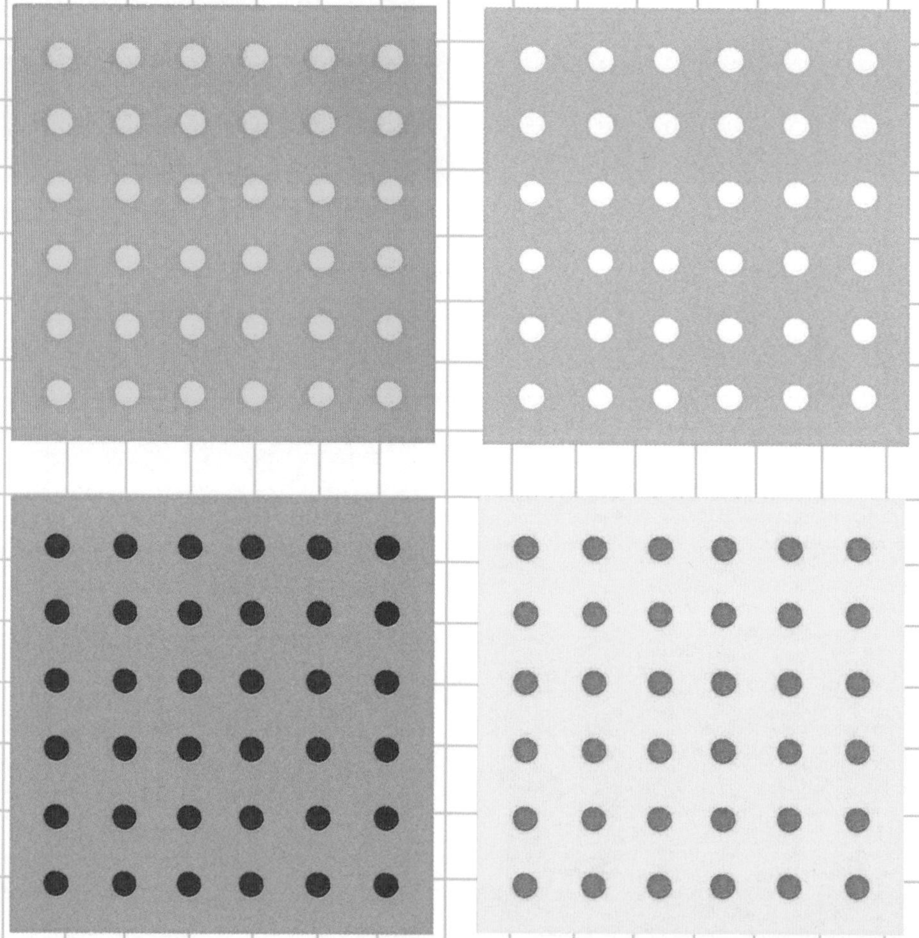

Boxes

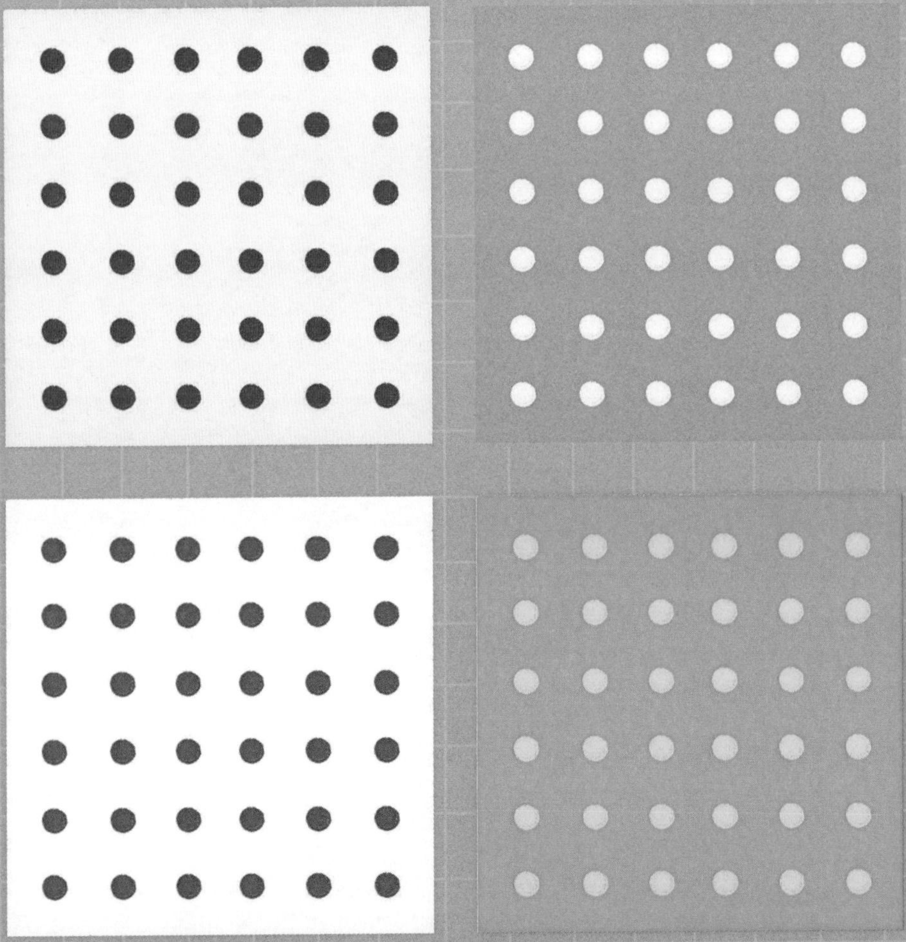

Boxes

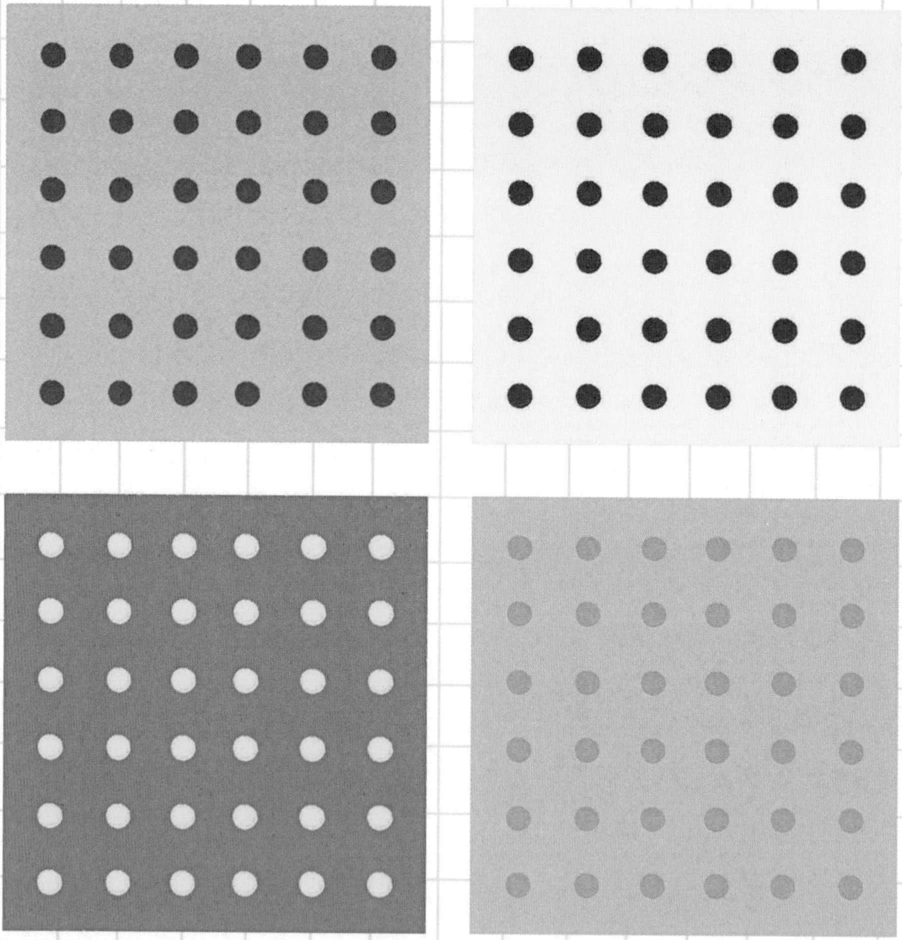

Triangles instructions

1. Player 1 (red) chooses one of the 'crosspoints' between the triangles, and draws a dot.

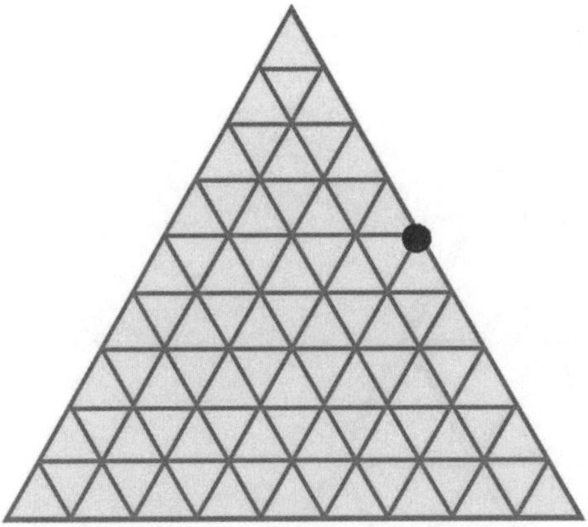

2. Player 2 (blue) then chooses one of the other crosspoints and draws a dot.

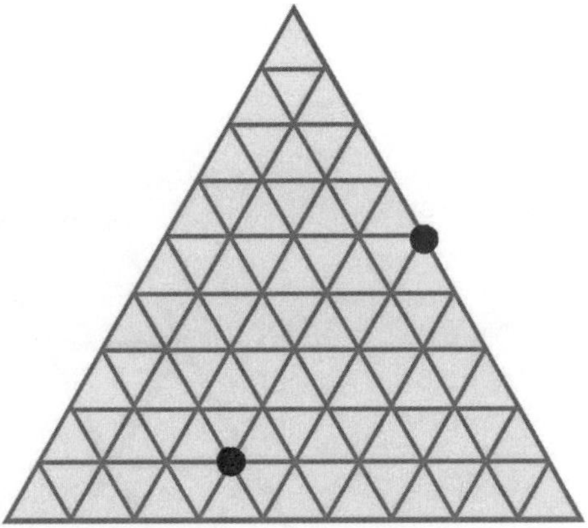

3. Take turns to mark crosspoints anywhere on the grid. Your goal is to make a chain that connects all three sides of the grid.

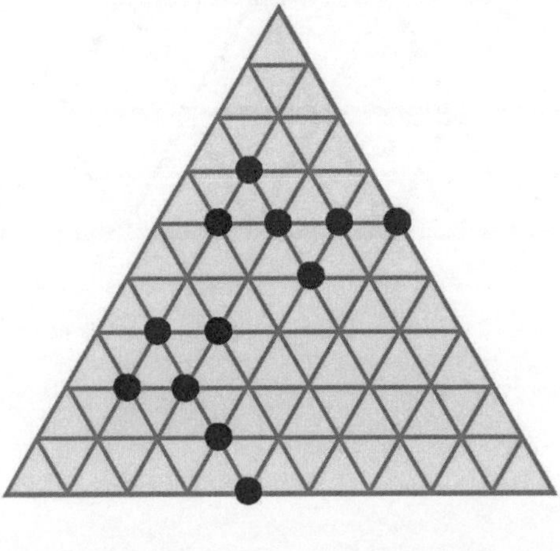

4. The winner is the first player to complete their chain. Player 1 won this game.

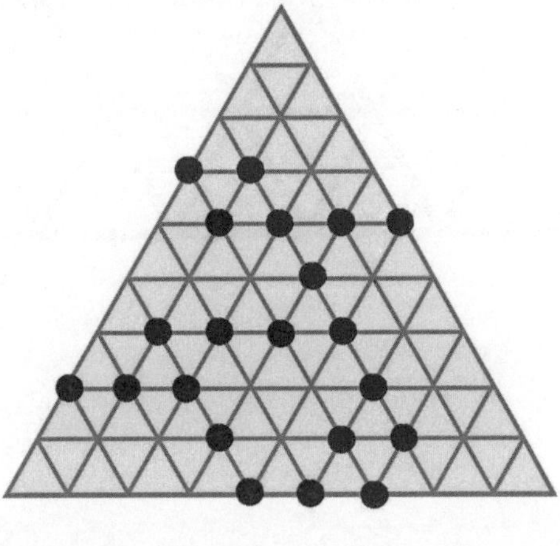

Triangles

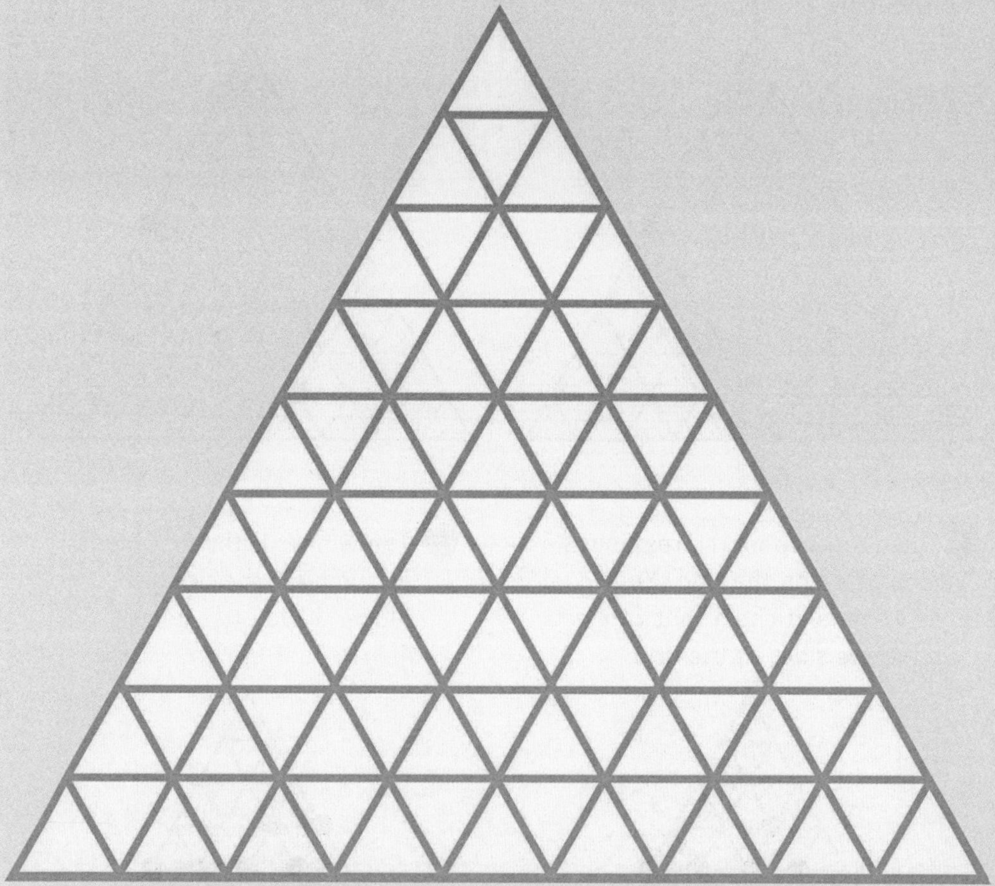

Triangles

Triangles

Triangles

Triangles

Triangles

Triangles

Triangles

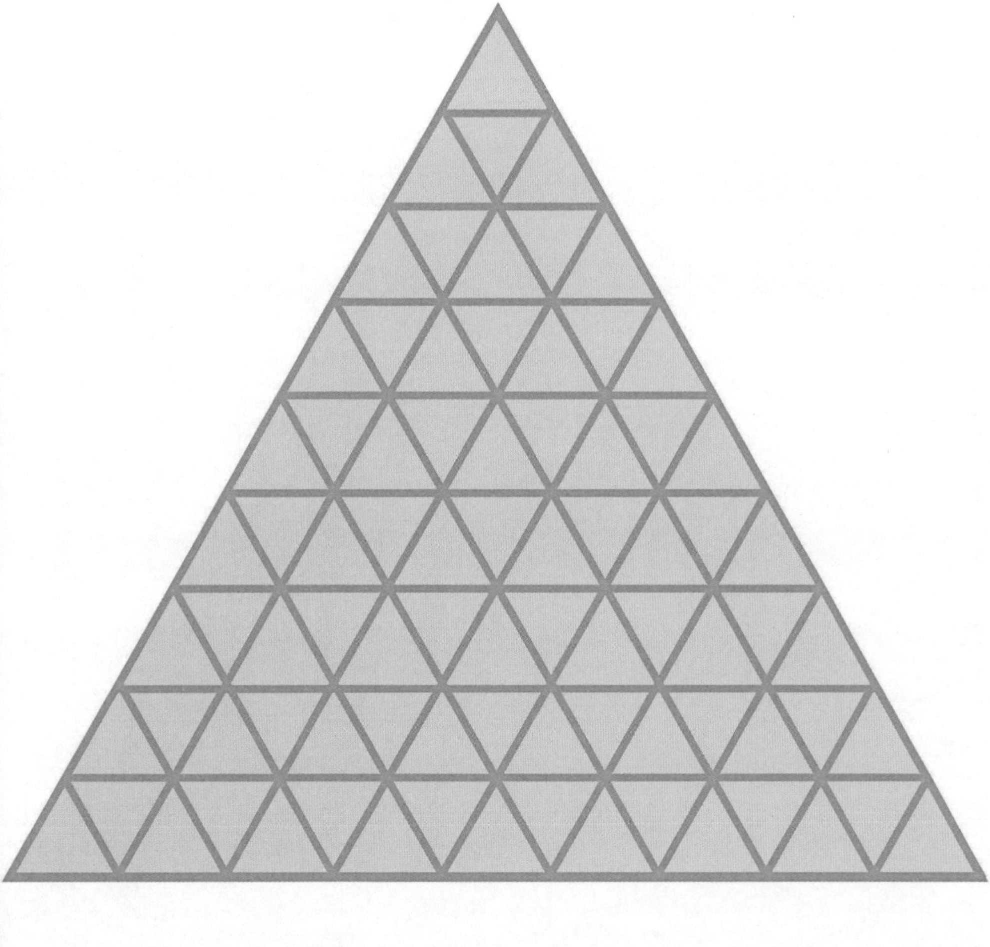

Triangles

Treasure hunter instructions

Before you start, cut or tear along the dotted line so you both have a map. Then secretly mark your treasure in one of the squares with an X.

1 Now take turns searching for your opponent's treasure. You can either guess the square it's on...

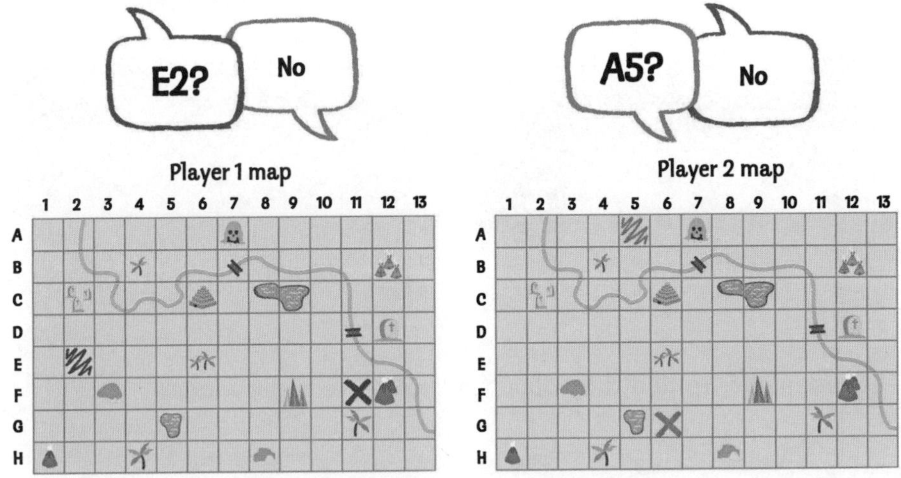

2 ...or ask a yes/no question to narrow the search.

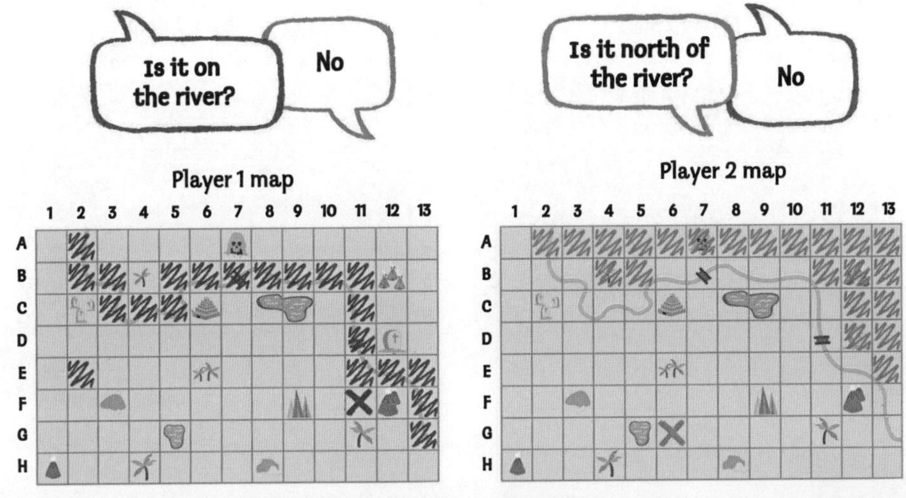

3 You can also use features on the map to help you in your search.

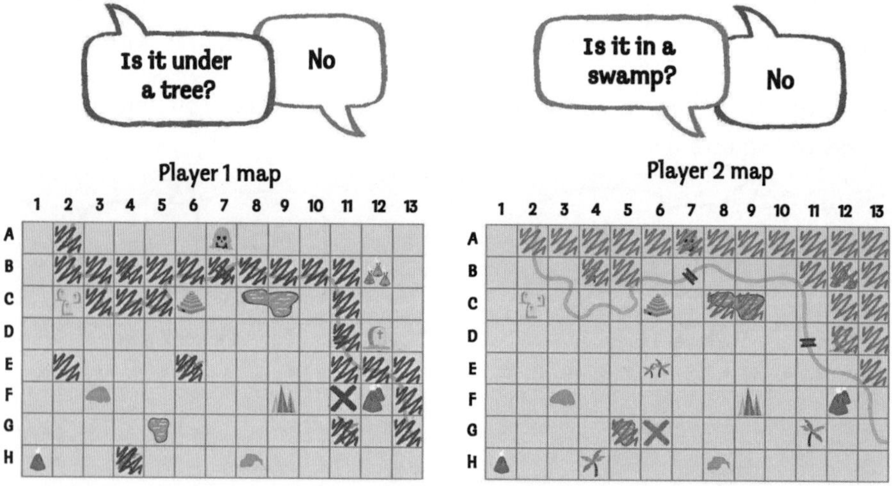

4 The first player to find their opponent's treasure is the winner.

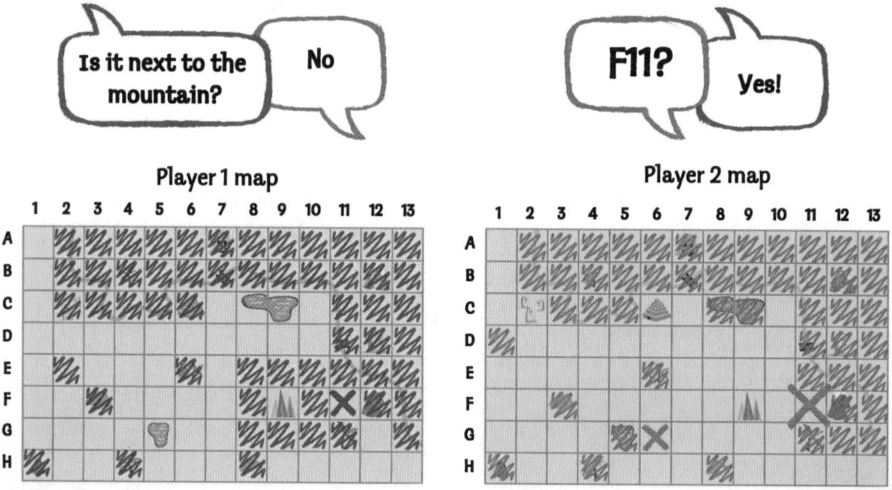

Treasure hunter

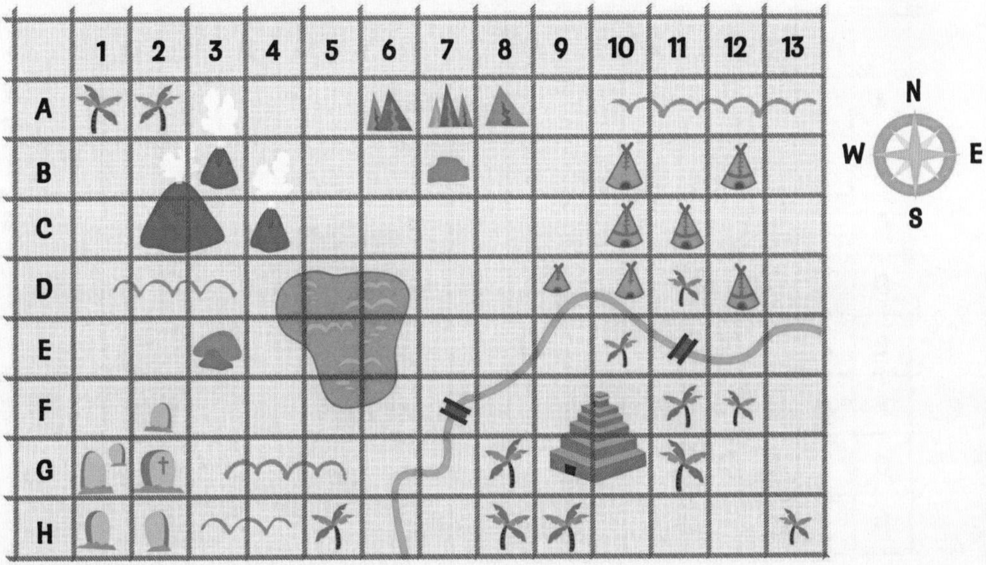

Cut or tear along the dotted line.

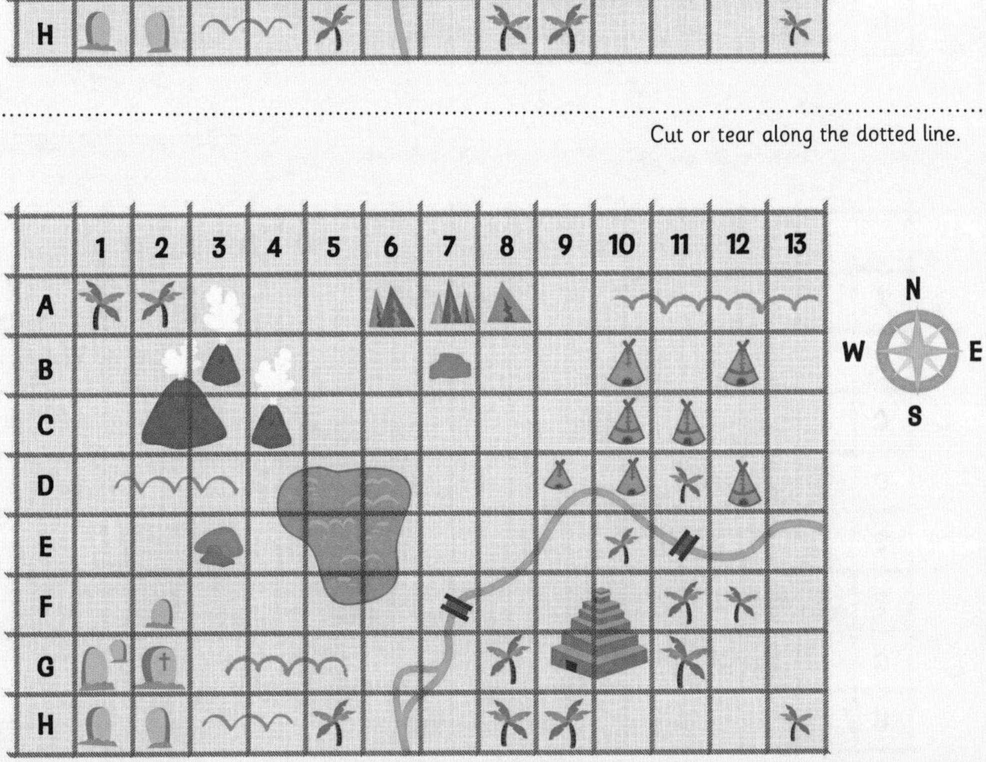

Treasure hunter

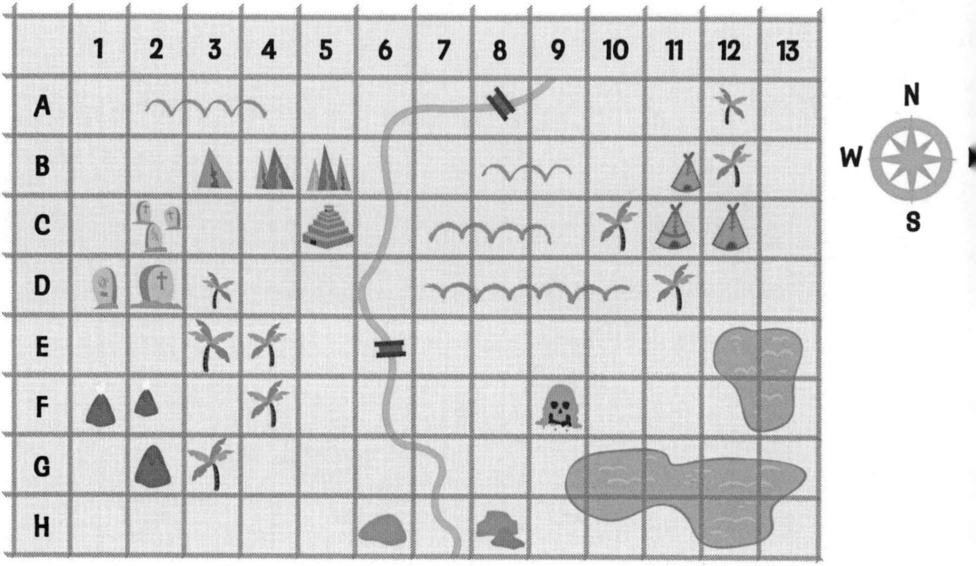

Cut or tear along the dotted line.

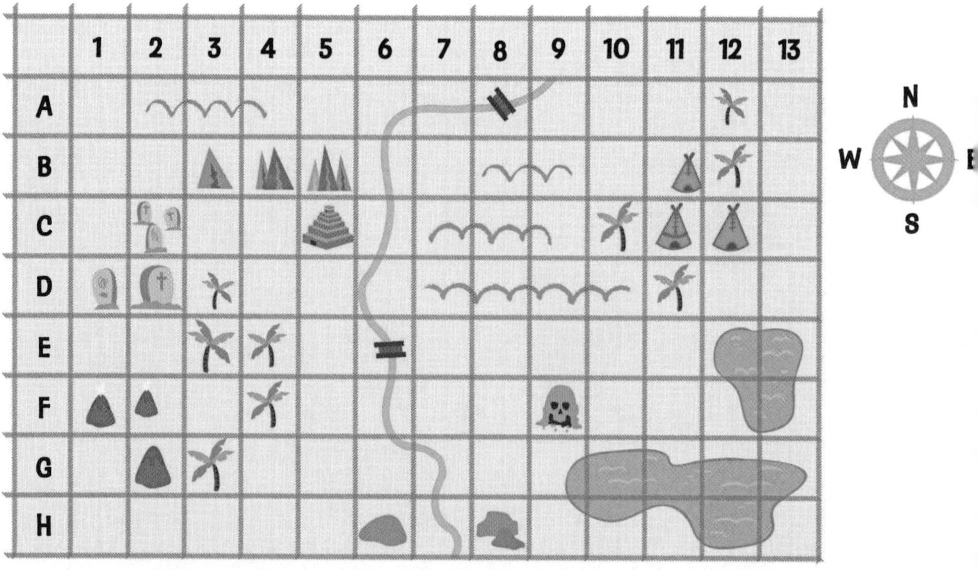

Treasure hunter

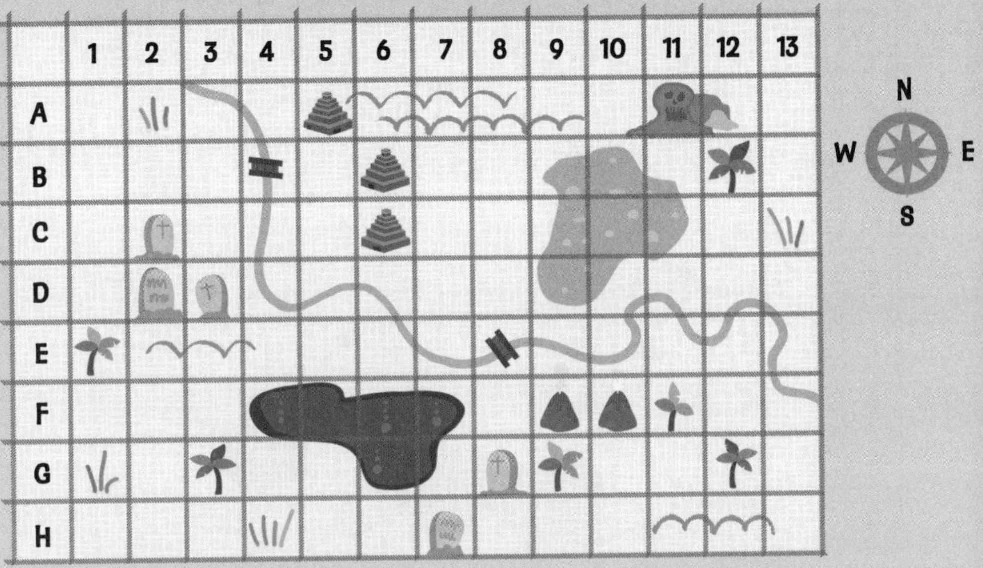

Cut or tear along the dotted line.

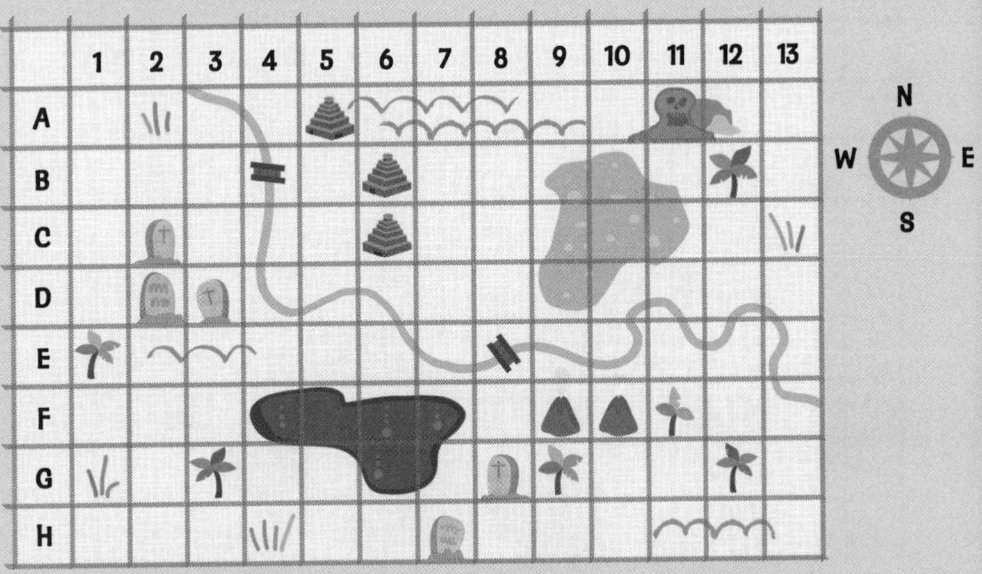

Treasure hunter

171

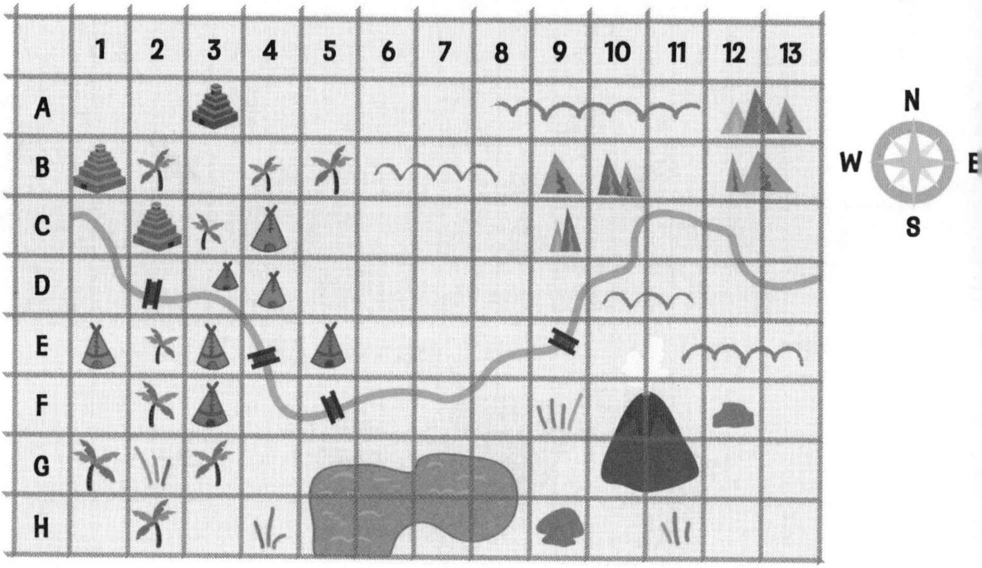

Cut or tear along the dotted line.

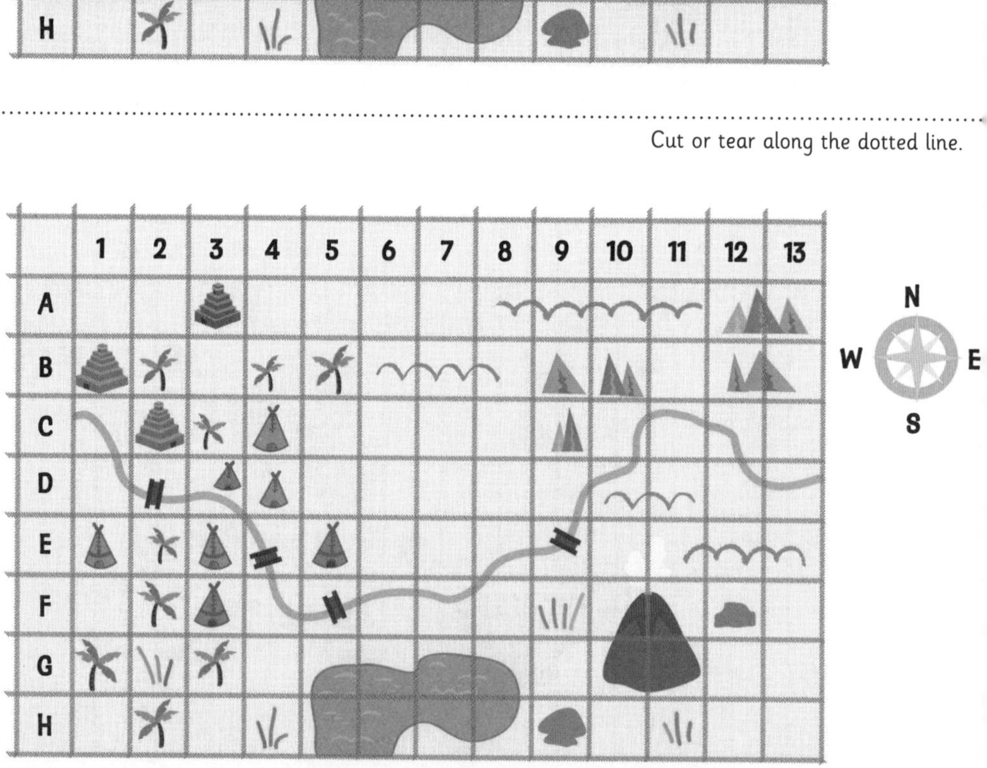

Treasure hunter

172

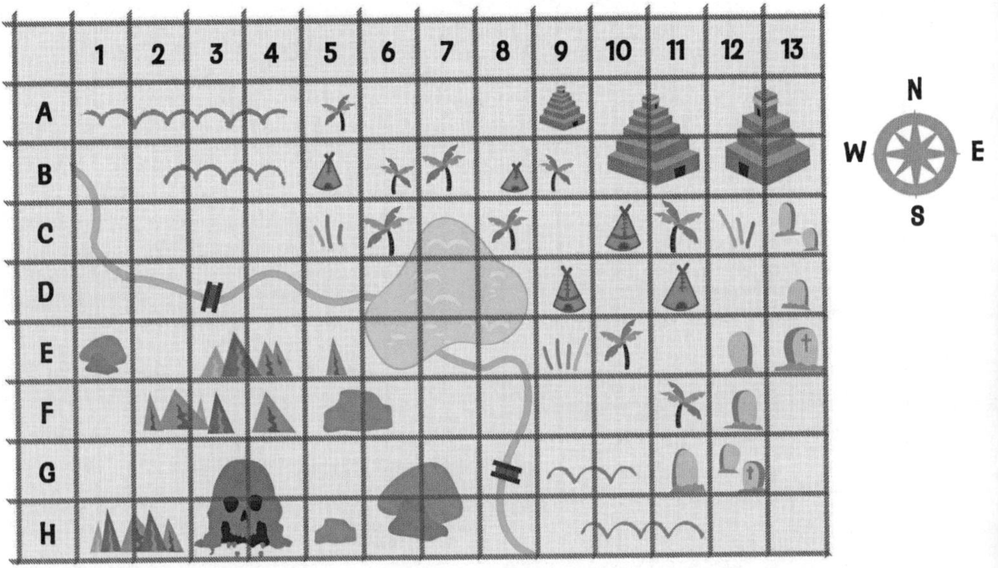

Cut or tear along the dotted line.

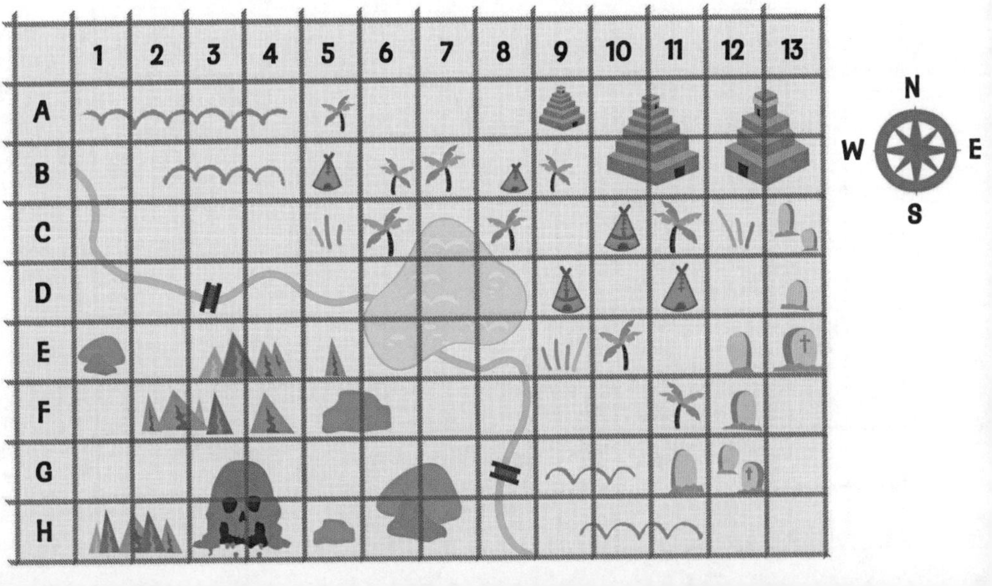

Treasure hunter

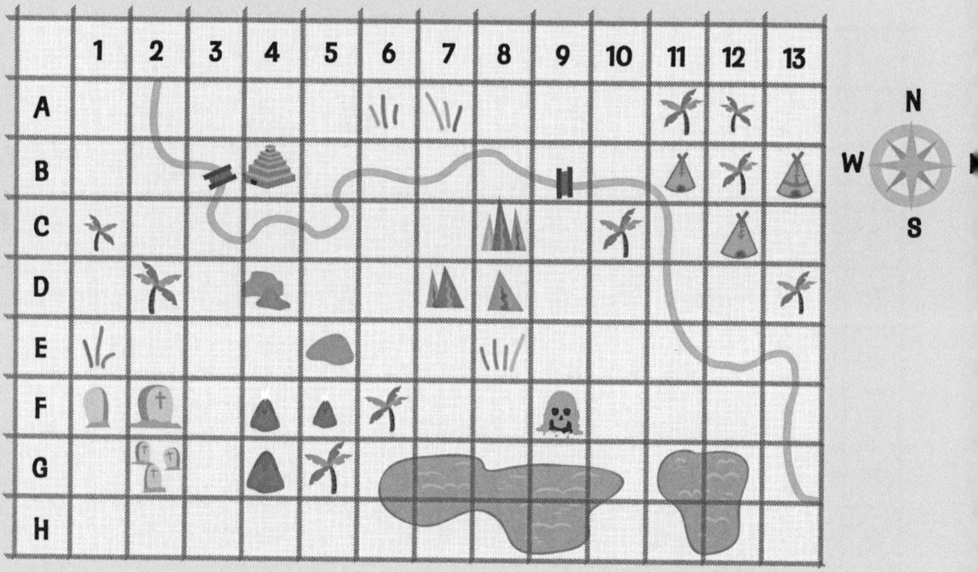

Cut or tear along the dotted line.

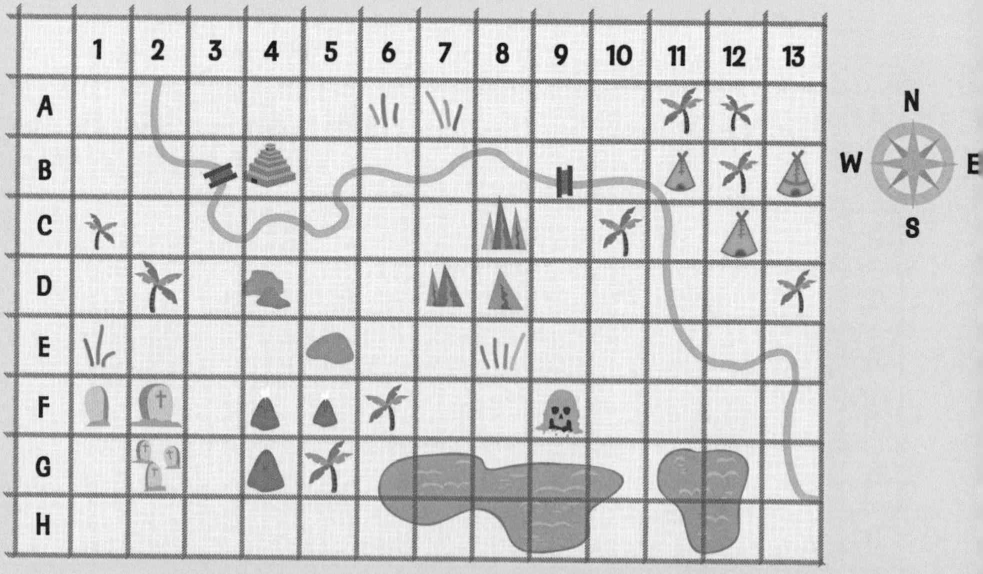

Treasure hunter

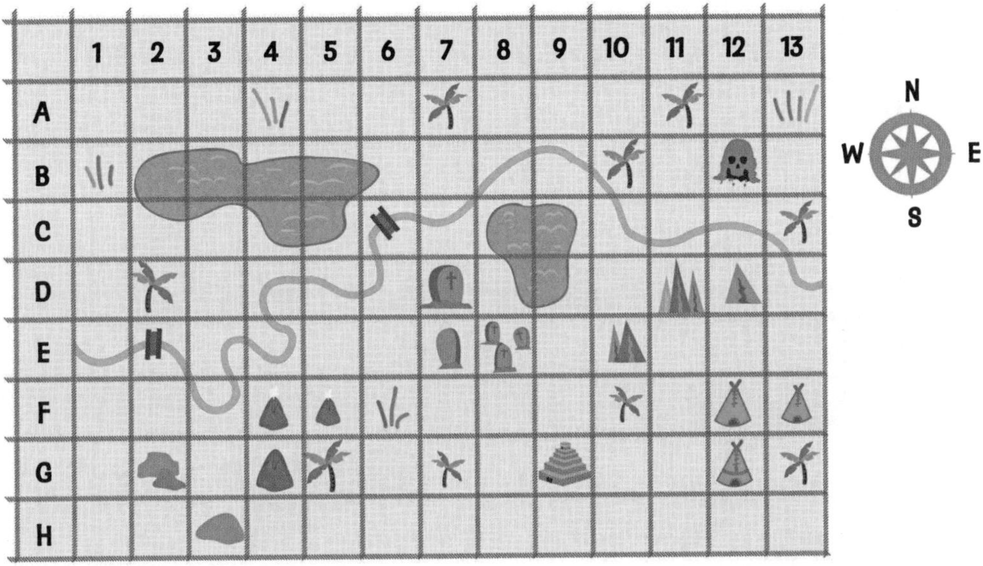

Cut or tear along the dotted line.

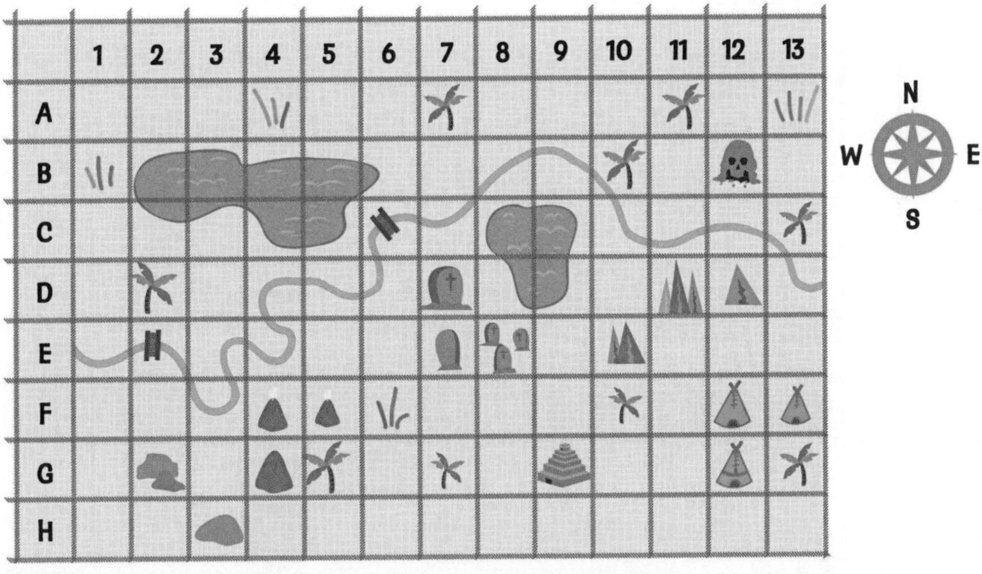

Treasure hunter

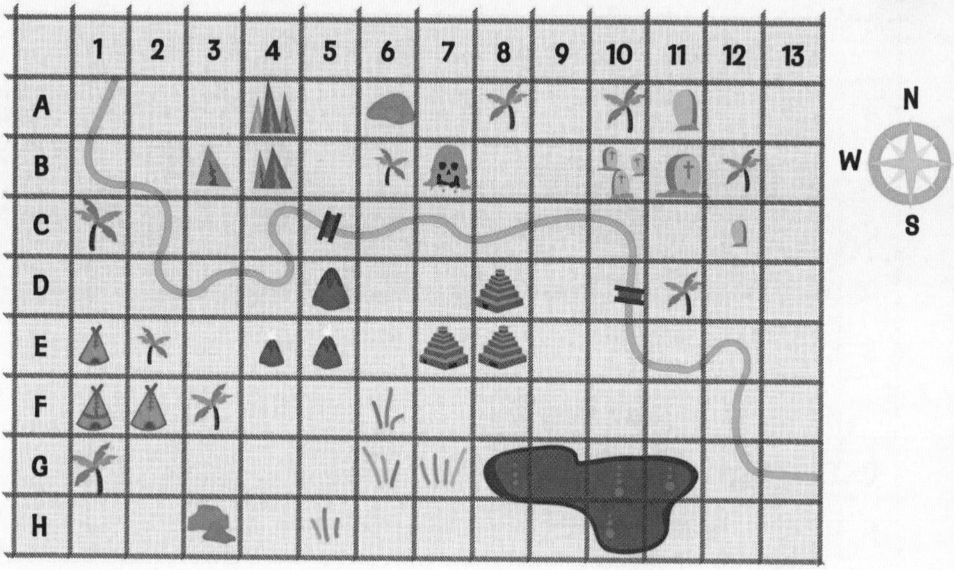

Cut or tear along the dotted line.

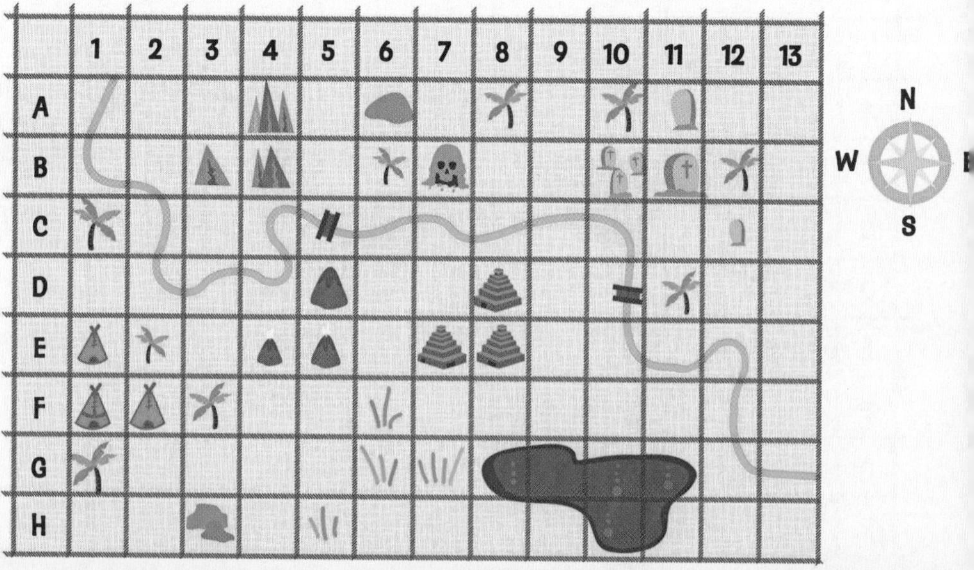

Sprouts instructions

1 Player 1 (blue): connect two of the dots, or draw a loop to connect a dot to itself, then add a new dot somewhere along the new line.

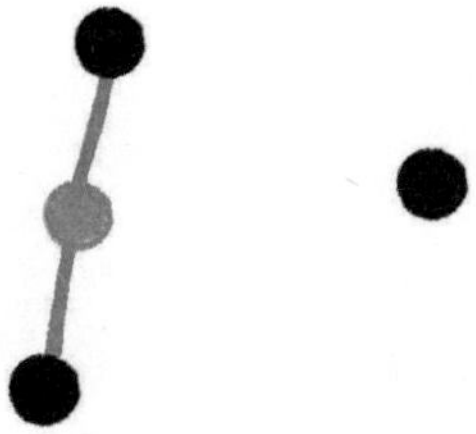

2 Player 2 (green): do the same. You can use the original dots, and also the new dot added by Player 1.

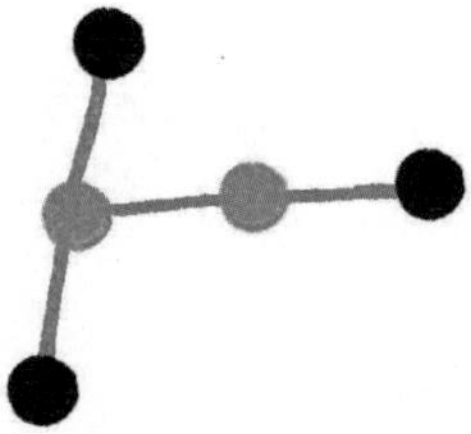

3 There are two things to remember: a dot can only have three lines coming out of it, and none of the lines can cross each other.

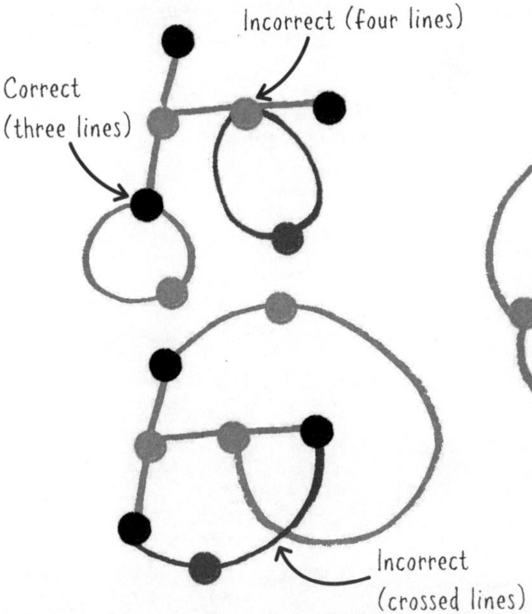

4 The loser is the first player who can't make a move. Player 1 won this game as Player 2 has nowhere to go.

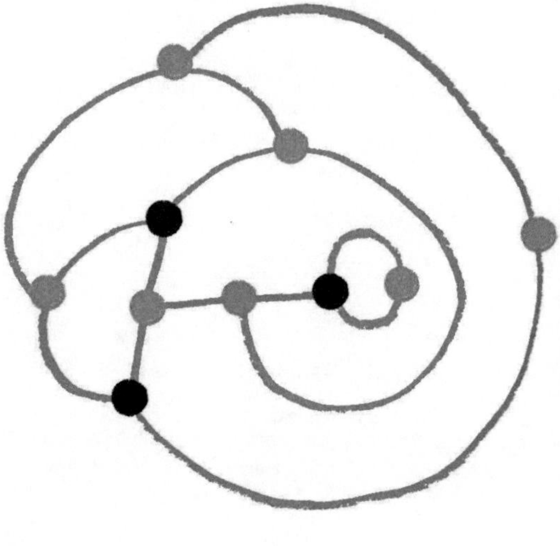

Sprouts

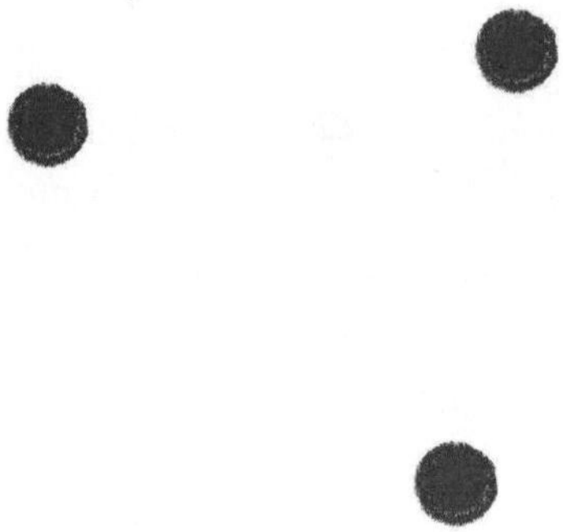

Sprouts

178

Sprouts

Sprouts

180

Sprouts

Sprouts

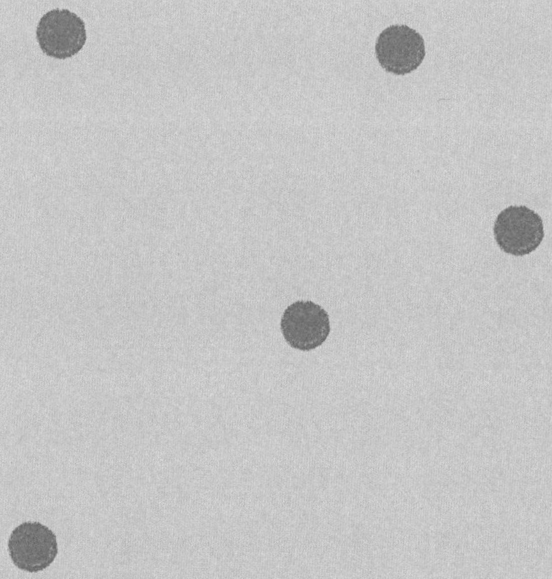

Sprouts

Sprouts

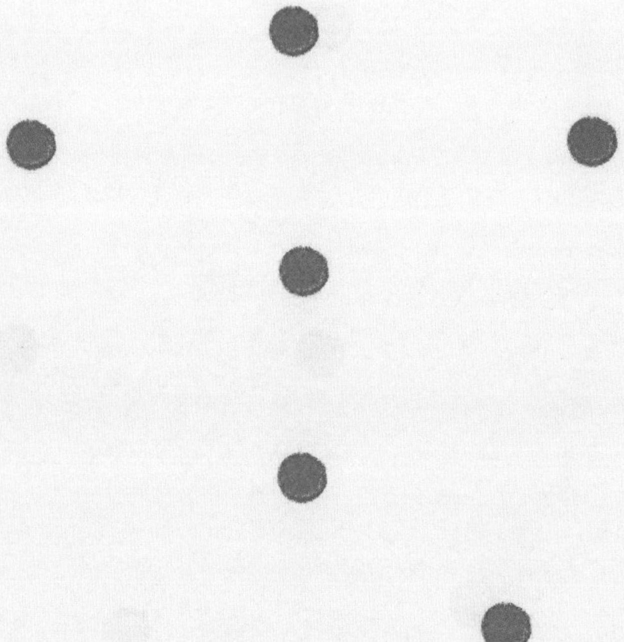

Sprouts

OXO instructions

1 Player 1 (black) and Player 2 take turns to mark an O or an X in empty squares on the grid. Both players can use either letter.

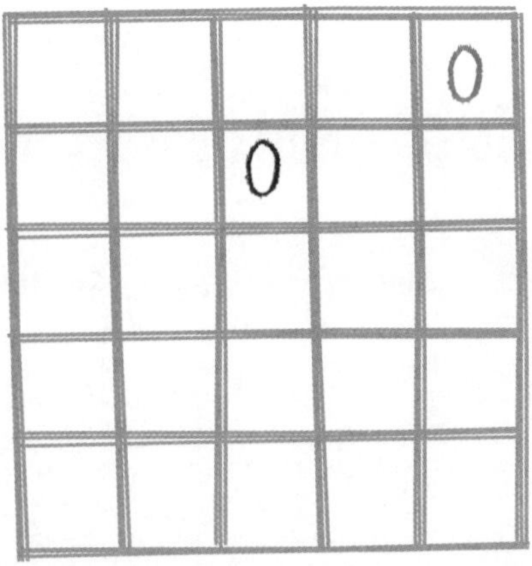

2 The goal is to complete lines that read 'OXO'. Player 1 has just completed a line by marking an O in the space below.

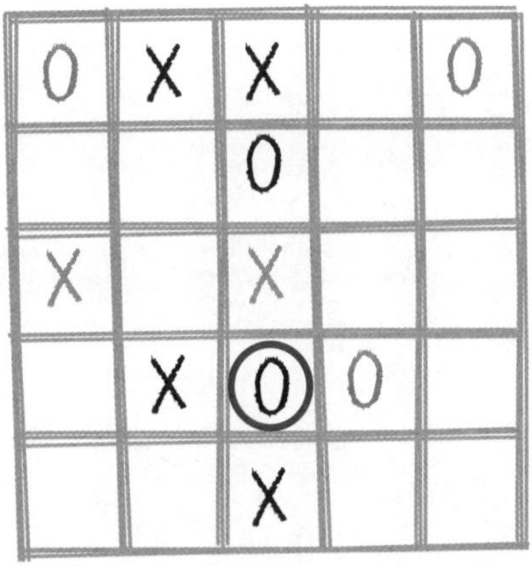

3 If you complete two lines with one letter, you get an extra turn. Player 2 has just completed two lines below.

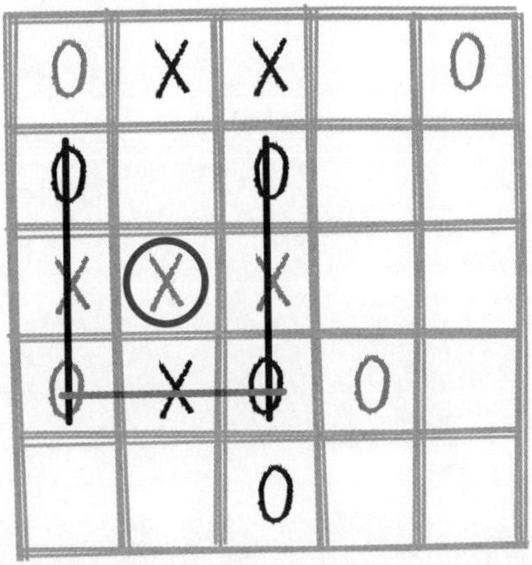

4 When all the spaces have been filled, the player who has completed the most lines is the winner. This game was a tie.

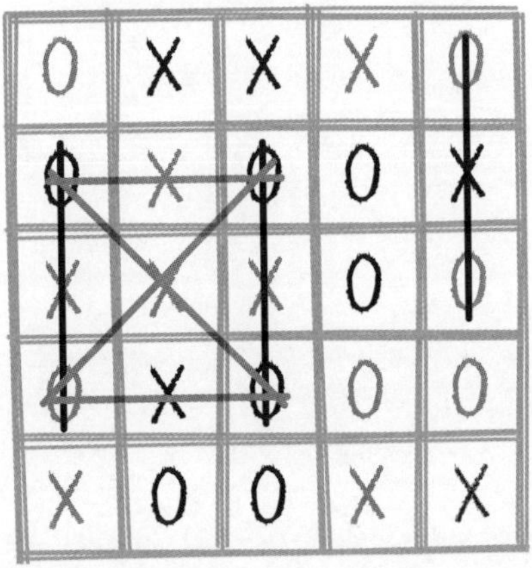

OXO

OXO

OXO

OXO

OXO

OXO

OXO

Pair them up instructions

1. Player 1 (blue) draws a line between any matching pair.

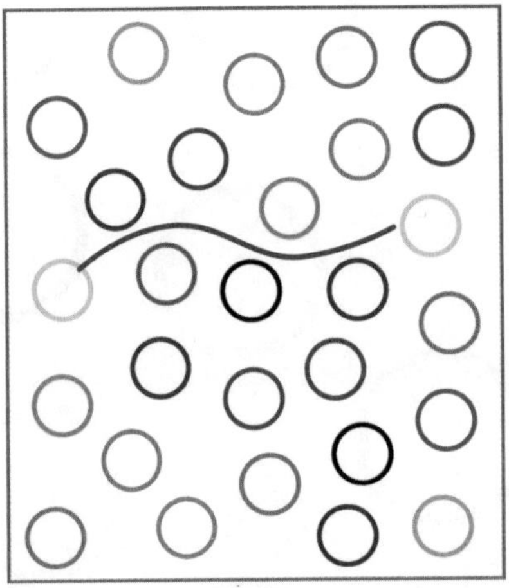

2. Player 2 (green) then draws a line between any other matching pair.

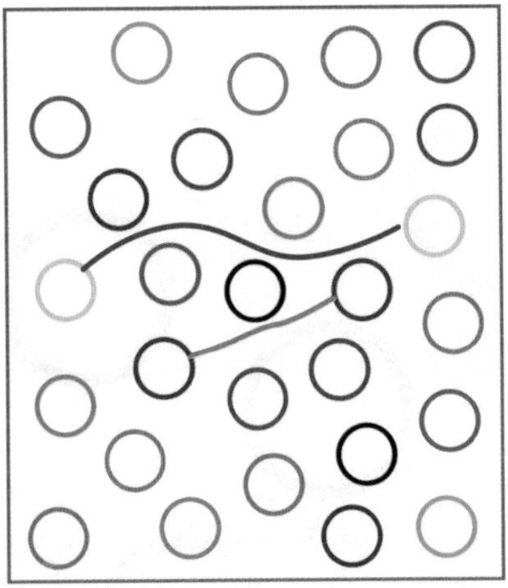

3. You must draw your line without taking your pen off the page. If it touches a circle from a different pair, or another line, you lose the game.

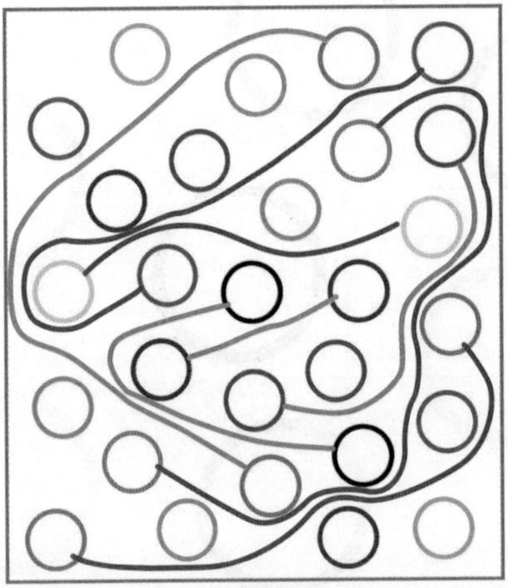

4. Player 2 won this game, because Player 1 touched another line while trying to join the two dark blue circles.

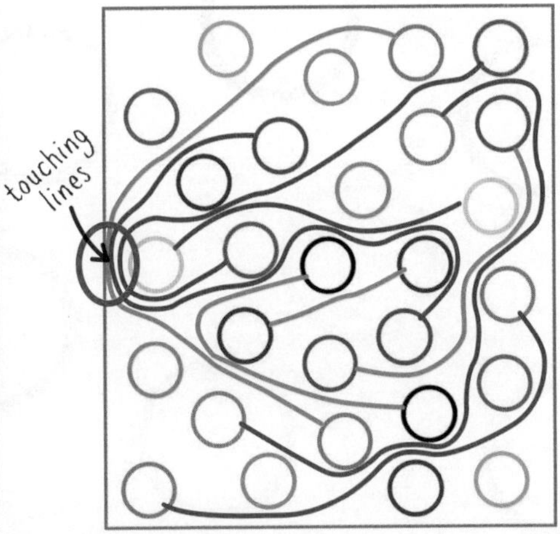

Pair them up

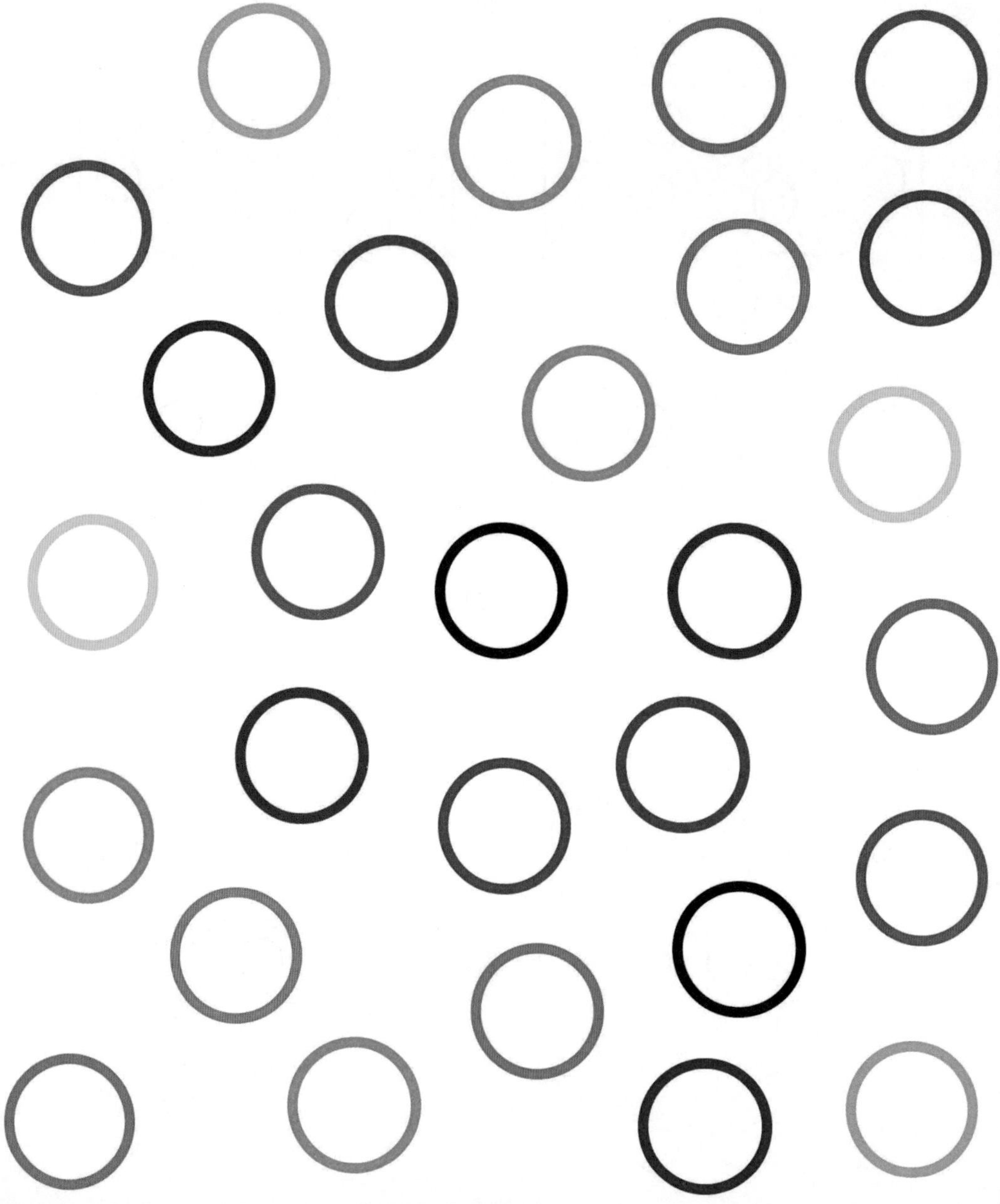

Pair them up

Pair them up

Pair them up

Pair them up

Pair them up

Pair them up